150 YEA
of a
HARTSHILL INSTITUTION

**The Story of
The Hartshill Workingmen's Institution
The Hartshill Church Institute
and
The Newcastle Players Theatre Workshop**

**by
Geoff Price**

First published 2009

Published by Geoffrey H. Price
103 Paris Avenue, Newcastle, Staffs. ST5 2QP
Email: geoff.price63@ntlworld.com

In association with The Newcastle Players
Email: newcastle.players@lineone.net
http://www.newcastleplayers.org.uk/

ISBN 978-0-9560653-2-2

Printed by Prontaprint Hanley
84 Piccadilly, Hanley
Stoke-on-Trent, ST 1 1HX

Photographs
by the author
unless credited otherwise

CONTENTS

APPENDICES

1. The Background

In 1969 The Newcastle Players acquired a building in Hartshill Road, Stoke-on-Trent originally called The Hartshill Workingmen's Institution and later The Hartshill Church Institute. For the past forty years or so the name over the door has been The Newcastle Players Theatre Workshop and since 1993 it has been a Grade II Listed Building.

In 2006 I and other Newcastle Players members had a meeting with representatives of the Heritage Lottery Fund, to investigate the possibility of obtaining funding for the renovation of the building. The outcome of the meeting, in brief, was that the Heritage Lottery Fund could not offer funding. One of the main stumbling blocks was that the Heritage Lottery Fund would require us to allow the public access to the building a certain number of times a year. Quite apart from the difficulty of providing staff to supervise such visits, there is also the problem that it is, as its present name suggests, a workshop and it houses theatrical scenery and properties in various stages of construction and a variety of tools and other equipment which, without protected viewing platforms or galleries for the visiting public – which the building does not have space for – could present a health and safety hazard.

On the other hand, we were told, the building is of obvious historical interest – hence its Listed Building status – and a book about its use over the years and other details would be of value. If we were to produce such a book, involving the local community in our research, the Heritage Lottery Fund might, it was suggested, assist with funding its publication.

The idea was not greeted with great enthusiasm at the time. The attention of most of those present at the meeting was focused more on carrying out the necessary renovation work and generating the necessary funding while at the same time dealing with the constantly ongoing work of preparing the sets for our two productions a year, which provide the main source of our income.

The book project was, therefore, put on hold. In 2006, though, I underwent surgery which was followed by some weeks of convalescence. I put the period of enforced physical inactivity to good use by writing and publishing a book which had been gestating in my mind for some considerable time. This was *Founded 1934 – The Story of The Newcastle Players* which went on sale at the end of 2006 with the profits going to the Workshop Refurbishment Fund.

It did not immediately lead on to the present book because, for one thing

I had no idea how to involve the local community.

The spur came in the form of a photograph published by our local newspaper, *The Sentinel*, in June 2007 in its *JIM MORGAN'S MYSTERY PICTURE* series. It showed Holy Trinity Church, Hartshill at some time in the 1940s viewed from the vicinity of what was then called The Hartshill Church Institute. The article accompanying the photograph provided clues to its location, "once a small hilltop village", and references to "the Victorian architect Gilbert Scott" and "an eminent potter who at that time lived in the parish". It asked readers to "guess where the photograph was taken".

In my letter, published in *The Sentinel* a week later, I identified the church and its location, adding that my interest was in the building on the other side of the road – the Institute – as I was planning to produce a history of it. I said that we had copies of newspaper articles published at the time it was officially opened and access to Newcastle Players documentation since 1969 when we acquired it. But, I said, there is a 111 year gap and I would be very grateful for any help *Sentinel* readers could give me in tracking down sources of information about the Hartshill Institute during the period from 1859 to 1969.

In September 2007 during the Heritage Open Days, a national event forming part of European Heritage Days, Burslem-based Urban Vision North Staffordshire Architecture and Urban Design Centre organised two guided walks in and around the old village of Hartshill led by local historian Andrew Dobraszczyc. Our workshop was included in these tours together with other buildings in the area such as Hartshill Church, the former Hartshill School and the Minton cottages. Many local residents said it was the first time they had been in the institute for over forty years and they expressed great interest in what we now use it for.

These tours and various items in *The Sentinel* produced quite a lot of anecdotal material about the use of the building for Brownies, Guides, Youth Club, Saturday night dances and so on, but very little in the way of hard evidence such as written matter or photographs. They did, however, provide contacts with Church Warden Chris Rushton and his wife Heather, through whom I gained access to copies of the parish magazine held in the Minton Centre (as the Church Hall is now called), Margaret Simpson, the current editor of both the parish magazine and the *Hartshill & Harpfields Residents' Association Newsletter* (see opposite page), and Angela Mountford, the current secretary of the Parochial Church Council.

Another valuable contact was local historian Richard Talbot who located information about the Institute in the late 1800s in his archives and pointed me in the direction of archival material held in the Staffordshire Record Office in Stafford. Other sources of information were Stoke-on-Trent City Archives at Hanley Library, Helen Burton of Keele University Library's Special

Hartshill & Harpfields
Residents' Association
Autumn 2008

Chair: Graham Simpson (Telephone 01782 614374)

From the chair...

The A.G.M. of Hartshill & Harpfields Residents Association will take place on Thursday 30th October 2008. The meeting will start at 7.30pm but doors will be open at 7.00pm to enable you to join us for a glass of wine. The first part of the meeting will be a police consutative meeting. Inspector Chris Harrington will be there together with other officials to bring local residents up to date on policing matters in the area. You will be able to raise any question direct with the officials. This will be followed immediately by the Residents' Association meeting.

Our Lady of the Angels & St Peter in Chains, Stoke

Parish Priest: Fr Thé-Quang
Deacon: Rev Mr Tony Bradshaw
Mass Times: Saturday Vigil 5.45 pm, Sunday 10.30 am
Mass times during the week: see notice board or website

Annual General Meeting

for all residents of Hartshill & Harpfields
Thursday 30th October at 7.30 pm in the Minton Community Centre, Minton Street. An opportunity to elect your committee, to find out what is happening in your neighbourhood and to let us have your views. • Join us at 7.00 pm for a glass of wine before the official AGM at 7.30 pm • Please support your Association

Hartshill Institute – 150th Anniversary

On Saturday 10th January 2009 it will be the 150th Anniversary of the official opening of the building known to many local people who grew up in the 30s, 40s, 50s and 60s as the Hartshill Church Institute. Since 1969 it has belonged to The Newcastle Players who renamed it The Newcastle Players Theatre Workshop.

To mark this important anniversary the Players will be holding an open evening on Saturday, 10th January and they are extending an invitation to anyone who remembers the Church Institute to come along and see what the building looks like now and to learn something about its current use.

Newcastle Players member Geoff Price has been researching the building's history and will shortly be publishing his book about it called *150 Years of a Hartshill Institution*. This will be your last chance to contribute your memories of activities there such as the Brownies, the Guides, the Youth Club, the Saturday night dances, the Hartshill Church Entertainers or even PT sessions as a pupil of Hartshill C. of E. Primary School. Photographs or other tangible memorabilia will be particularly welcome.

The Open Evening will be from 7.30 p.m. and 9.30 p.m. Admission will be free.

Margaret Simpson, the editor of both the Hartshill Parish Magazine and the Hartshill & Harpfields Residents' Association Newsletter (above), has been very helpful in tracking down memories of the Hartshill Church Institute.

Residents of Hartshill and other interested parties listen to local historian Andrew Dobraszczyc – in the rather cramped conditions of the partly constructed set for the Newcastle Players production of "Billy Liar" – on Thursday, 6th September 2007 during a guided tour of buildings in Hartshill connected with the Minton family as part of the 2007 National Heritage Open Days.

Collections and Archives, Royal Doulton Archivist Les Smith, Terry Millington of St John Ambulance and Andrew Dobraszczyc's tutorial notes – *The Minton Family & Stoke* and *The Minton Family & Hartshill* – written to accompany two of his Social History Walks for Keele University.

The local media in the form of *The Sentinel*, which I have already mentioned, and *BBC Radio Stoke* have been very helpful in publicising my search for information.

Three others I should thank are: Roger Jones for research into the 1861 census; Pat Mason for providing various items from the local press in the 1850s and 1860s which he unearthed while seeking information in support of our National Lottery application referred to in Chapter 10; and Graham Yelland who restored the photograph of Hartshill Guides on page 38.

Finally I would like to thank everybody who has provided me with snippets of information – of various sizes – which have contributed to this book and, last but not least, my wife Mary who has patiently endured the many months I have devoted to this project.

2. Herbert Minton and Colin Minton Campbell

Herbert Minton and his nephew Colin Minton Campbell were prominent figures in 19th century Stoke and Hartshill. In Stoke Herbert Minton built up and expanded the pottery manufacturing business started earlier in the century by his father Thomas Minton. In the 1840s – the exact year varies from account to account – he took his wife's nephew Michael Daintry Hollins into partnership and, a few years later, his own nephew Colin Minton Campbell. By the time of Herbert Minton's death in 1858 the firm was the largest employer in the town. At first Hollins and Minton continued the partnership but, after five years, they split up, Hollins taking over the tile works and Campbell retaining the earthenware and china works.

Colin Minton Campbell also played a major role in the public life of the town of Stoke-upon-Trent and, amongst other things, he served as its mayor in 1880, 1881 and 1882. In 1883 he refused to stand for re-election, pleading ill health and the pressure of work. He died two years later.

The site of the former Minton factory is now occupied by a Sainsbury superstore, but it has not entirely lost its connection with the Minton name, since a statue of Colin Minton Campbell by the sculptor Thomas Brock has been restored by the Sainsbury company and now stands outside the store looking across the road to the Herbert Minton Building (Headquarters of the Stoke on Trent Primary Care Trust). The Brock statue originally stood in Campbell Place where it was unveiled by the Duchess of Sutherland in January 1887 reportedly in front of a crowd of 10,000 people. It was later moved to Kingsway and then, in 1954, to a site outside the Minton factory's office block in what is now Fleming Road. It was re-erected just around the corner outside the Sainsbury store in March 2003. The Herbert Minton Building was built in 1877 on land given by Colin Minton Campbell, who is described on the statue's plinth as A SUCCESSFUL MANUFACTURER, A LEADING TOWNSMAN AND GENEROUS FRIEND.

Hartshill, up the hill on the road from Stoke to Newcastle, was where Herbert Minton and Colin Minton Campbell lived with their families and spent their leisure time. There is much to remember them both by in Hartshill.

The Brock statue of Colin Minton Campbell photographed in 1996 outside the Minton office block in Fleming Road, Stoke.

John Ward's book *The Borough of STOKE-UPON-TRENT* published in 1843 briefly mentions "Cliff Bank Lodge, a handsome villa, recently erected by Thomas Garrett, Esq., resident partner of the firm of Copeland and Garrett" and then goes on as follows:

Half a mile further, on the road to Newcastle, at Harts Hill, is Long-field Cottage, the unassuming but elegant seat of Herbert Minton, Esq., one of the opulent manufacturers of Stoke. It is a neat residence, and has another house near it of corresponding character. Mr. Minton is the active patron of religious education, and not only maintains a day-school for the children of his workpeople in the Town of Stoke, but has erected near his house school-rooms for the instruction of the children in that populous vicinity. He has also commenced the building of a church on the neighbouring eminence, which, when reared to its intended height, will form a prominent and graceful object to the whole superficies of the Borough, displayed like a panorama from this elevated spot to singular advantage. The church is of stone, in the Gothic style of architecture, and calculated to accommodate nearly 1,000 persons. It will be endowed wholly by the benevolent founder, who is, at the same time, building a parsonage house, of corresponding style, close by.

The church was designed by the architect George Gilbert Scott – later Sir George Gilbert Scott – one of the leading members of the British Gothic Revival, who is probably best known nationally for St Pancras Station and the Albert Memorial in London. In neighbouring Cheshire he directed major restoration work at Sandbach Parish Church between 1847 and 1849; he designed the original buildings for Sandbach School on its present site in 1849; and in 1857 he designed Sandbach Literary Institute.

At about the same time he was engaged by Herbert Minton to design the Minton Cottages, a row of eight houses plus two separate detached houses at each end on the opposite side of the road to Hartshill Church. The detached houses (now numbers 263 and 285 Hartshill Road) housed managers at the Minton factories and the other eight (numbers 267 to 281 – there is no 265 or 283) housed workers at the factories. The project was conceived by Herbert Minton but he died before it could be completed.

Minton's death was reported in *The Staffordshire Advertiser* of Saturday, 3rd April 1858 and a shorter version of the article was reprinted in *The Times* of 6th April. Although his life and achievements were reported in glowing terms, they were not glowing enough for *Times* reader E.L. of East Sheen who felt he had to write to the editor to add his own tribute – albeit with a dubious figure for the number of children the schools could accommodate:

Sir, – Gratified as every friend of the late Mr. Minton must be on perusing the notice of him which appeared in *The Times* of yesterday, you will I hope allow me to mention a proof of his great benevolence and charity, and which cannot be too extensively made known, for it has few parallels.

From his own private resources Mr. Minton built a beautiful church in the hamlet in which he lived, near Stoke-upon-Trent, and adorned it with a fine spire, stained-glass windows, and organ, and appropriate seats – a pattern of architectural good taste which might well be copied. He erected near the church schools for 1,500 boys and girls, with houses for a master and mistress, providing for their maintenance and the education of the children. He also built a very commodious parsonage-house for a resident clergyman, adding to it a good garden and some land, and amply endowed his new living. He had it in contemplation to erect and endow several almshouses for his aged workmen, but I am not aware whether they have yet been completed.

These good deeds ought to be known not only as affording a proof of Mr. Minton's desire to improve the spiritual welfare of his fellow-creatures, but of his active benevolence. His disposition, sweetness of temper, and strong good sense made him beloved by his friends and universally esteemed and admired both by rich and poor in, his own neighbourhood.

I am, &c.

East Sheen, April 7. E.L.

The Minton Cottages were completed after Herbert Minton's death by Colin Minton Campbell, who went on to finance four more cottages (numbers 289 to 295 Hartshill Road) and the building (number 287 Hartshill Road) that is the subject of this book. It is now known as The Newcastle Players Theatre Workshop, but before that it was called The Hartshill Church Institute and originally The Hartshill Working Men's Institution.

There is more on the subject of the Herbert Minton and Colin Minton Campbell in Andrew Dobraszczyc's tutorial notes: *The Minton Family & Stoke* and *The Minton Family & Hartshill* and there are some excellent photographs of the Minton Cottages at www.thepotteries.org. Just type Minton Cottages in the search box.

3. Location

T he address of the building we call The Newcastle Players Theatre Workshop is – and always has been as long as the Newcastle Players have owned it – 287 Hartshill Road, Stoke-on-Trent, ST4 7NQ, although what its address was when it was built in 1858 is not clear. The name of the road has been changed at least once and so has the numbering of the buildings in it.

The report of the official opening which appeared in *The Staffordshire Sentinel* of 15 January 1859 describes the front of the Hall forming "a gable to the Newcastle Road." Yet the relevant sheets of the 1861 census, just two years later, appear to refer to the road as Hartshill or Harts Hill.

By the time the 1869 edition of *Keates' Gazetteer & Directory of the Staffordshire Potteries, Newcastle and District* was published the name of the road was Stoke Road and according to the Ordnance Survey maps of the area it kept that name until at least 1900. On the 1924 OS map, however, it is shown with its present name of Hartshill Road.

As regards the numbering of the various buildings, the 1861 census merely lists the occupants names with the Working Men's Institution shown between the houses occupied by Thomas Oakden and his family (now No. 285) and Thomas Hill and his wife Rebecca (now No. 289).

At some stage numbers were introduced, but originally without any obvious logic. The 1955 edition of Barrett's *Directory of the City of Stoke-on-Trent* shows the detached house at the Stoke end of the Minton Cottages (now No. 263) as No. 317. The eight cottages (now 267 to 281) were numbered 325 to 339, in other words a similar sequence of odd numbers but with three numbers missing between 317 and 325. The current numbers 285 and 289, which are on either side of the former Institute, were numbered 347 and 357, so this time there was even larger gap in the numbering.

Barrett's *Directory of the City of Stoke-on-Trent* gives the current numbers in its 1958 edition but what our building was numbered before it became 287 is anybody's guess, as the relevant large scale Ordnance Survey maps do not show house numbers.

In 1938 Stoke-on-Trent City Council widened Hartshill Road outside the

The Newcastle Players Theatre Workshop with two of the Campbell Cottages on the right and one of the Minton Cottages on the left seen from the end of Vicarage Road. The corner of the Jolly Potters Inn is on the left of the picture.

Institute and the Minton Cottages. Even a 16 feet to 1 inch sketch map prepared in this connection by the City Engineer and Surveyor shows no numbers, just the name Hartshill Church Institute with the "Jolly Potters" Inn diagonally opposite at the corner of Vicarage Road with a note "from Newcastle" on the left and another "to Stoke" on the right.

Nowadays we tell people they can find The Newcastle Players Theatre Workshop about half-way between The Jolly Potters and the Tesco Express on the other side of the road. The Tesco store is a fairly recent addition to the Hartshill landscape but The Jolly Potters was built in about 1830 and it became a beerhouse a few years later. It was in fact the sort of place that Colin Minton Campbell and his associates were trying to keep working men out of with the building of the Hartshill Working Men's Institution.

4. The Hartshill Working Men's Institution

In January of 1856 "a few philanthropic individuals desirous of promoting the moral and social welfare of their less favoured neighbours" – to quote *The Staffordshire Advertiser* of Saturday, 26th January – decided to form an institution "to promote the moral and intellectual improvement of the working-classes, by means of a reading room, class instructions, lectures, and meetings for discussion." They called it the Hartshill Working Men's Association and the newspaper article reported:

> At a preliminary meeting, held a few days ago, 65 members were enrolled; Herbert Minton, Esq., was appointed president; the Rev. W. D. Isaac, vice-president; Colin Minton Campbell, Esq., treasurer; and Mr Snelson, secretary. The opening lecture will be delivered on Monday evening, by the vice-president. The newsroom, which will be supplied with seven daily and eighteen weekly newspapers, as well as leading periodicals, will be opened on the following day; and there will be classes for reading, writing, arithmetic, grammar, geography, &c. We are glad to see that the plan of the committee also embraces a provision for rational amusements. The terms of the membership are 4d per month.

Although the original idea for this association probably came from Herbert Minton, the driving force behind it was Colin Minton Campbell and he was undoubtedly responsible for the setting up of the Hartshill Working Men's Association. Herbert Minton was appointed president but he had retired from the family firm and was preparing to move to Torquay so he played no active role in the organisation. After his death in 1858 Colin Minton Campbell took over as president.

The association had its ups and downs. Campbell and his associates had subscribed to all the best daily and weekly papers of the time and most of the best periodicals. They also started to set up a library and hoped that before long they would have "a large collection of the most useful and interesting works of the day". They had also commenced a class for the working men, but unfortunately it did not last, because the men were driven out by the boys of the parish, who came in such numbers that the men had no room, and retired, he supposed, in disgust. It appears that the boys soon lost interest, but by then the damage was done.

On the other hand, in its issue of Saturday, 21st June 1856 *The Staffordshire Advertiser* reported that the "HARTSHILL HORTICULTURAL SOCIETY, CONNECTED WITH THE WORKING MEN'S ASSOCIATION – President, The Rt. Hon. the Earl of Harrowby" would be holding its first "Grand Horticultural and Floricultural Exhibition" in the Hartshill Schoolrooms on the following Thursday (26th June). There would be three classes of prizes awarded to the Exhibitors: "the first to be competed for by Gentlemen's Gardeners and Nurserymen; the second by Amateurs; and the third by Cottagers." The price of admission would be one shilling from 2 till 4 and sixpence from 4 till 7. A tent for refreshments would be erected near the schoolrooms.

In his tutorial notes entitled *The Minton Family and Hartshill* Andrew Dobraszczyc draws the conclusion that these admission charges were designed to separate the gentry, who could attend in the afternoon, from the working classes, who were expected to come in the evening.

By early 1858 the entertainment provided by the association was proving more successful. *The Staffordshire Sentinel* of 16th January 1858 reported that what it described as "The cheap entertainments in connection with the above institution", i.e. the Working Men's Association, "seem to be more appreciated than at first, judging by the highly respectable audience on Monday evening last." There were songs by Miss Heath, Messrs Goodwin and Leason, while Mr Bentley "presided at the piano-forte" and "Mr. T. Cartledge's quadrille band contributed to the harmony of the evening". There were readings by Mr Edgar "who gave some choice pieces from Robert Burns" and Mr R. Leason, the latter reading an original paper on General Havelock and giving a recitation called "The Field of Waterloo" from Byron's *Childe Harold*. The paper commented that "the evening's entertainment was evidently much appreciated by all present, if we may judge from the hearty manner in which the various pieces were received" and it added that there would be no entertainment on the following Monday, as the association's Annual Tea Party, its second, would be taking place on the Tuesday evening.

This was reported at length in the local press. *The Staffordshire Sentinel* of 23rd January 1858, for example, contains the following article on the annual tea meeting and concert, which is roughly double the length of a front page article in today's *Sentinel.* Paragraph breaks have been added to make it easier to read in the 21st century:

HARTSHILL WORKING MEN'S ASSOCIATION. – The second annual tea meeting and concert in connection with the above association, was held in the Hartshill School Rooms, on Tuesday evening last. The attendance was good, there being 250 present during tea, that number being largely augmented at the concert which followed.

C M. Campbell, Esq., presided, and, previous to the commencement of the concert, made a few introductory remarks, in the course of which he observed that the Provident Society, which he told them last year was going to be started, in connection with the association, had been very successful. During the year £60 had been deposited, and although, on one occasion as much as £5 had been paid in at once, yet the bulk of that amount had been invested in various sums from 1d up to £1, but out of the £60 so deposited, only £10 now remained in the name of the society; as when one had saved £1 10s it became invested in their own name in the Savings Bank, and was entirely under the control of the depositor.

Mr R. Leason, secretary, then read the annual report, from which we learnt that the association was, upon the whole, going on satisfactorily, and, having passed the first blush of novelty, might now be considered as having steadily entered on a career of increasing usefulness. The number of members, at the present time, was 100. Classes for instruction in various departments of knowledge, had been carried on throughout the year, the attendance being very good. Recently, the committee had established weekly reading and musical entertainments, which had also proved very successful. The reading room had been supplied with newspapers and periodicals, the attendance showing how well that department of this institution was appreciated. The horticultural branch of the association, last summer, held three shows, which were also very successful, being attended by a great number of visitors, and F. Tomlinson, Esq. was so much pleased with the amount of emulation which his prize had awakened amongst the cottagers, that he had promised to continue it another year. It was the intention of the committee to hold two horticultural shows during the current year; the first on the 11th of May, and the other on the 6th of August. The Provident Society had also been successful, £60 having been paid in during the year. The total amount of subscriptions for the year was £54 14s 4d. The expenditure had been £53 15s 9d, leaving a balance in the hands of the treasurer of 18s 7d. The receipts on account of the horticultural branch had been £87 13s, and the expenditure £88 19s, so that in this department there was a balance due to the treasurer of £1 6s.

The concert which succeeded was of a very interesting character, the vocalists being Miss Bentley and Miss Heath, Messrs T. Griffiths, L. Watkin, W. Polgrean, W. Leason, J. Newton, and T. L. Emery; the latter of whom also presided at the pianoforte. Master W. Jones, of Stoke, also played two solos on the concertina with good effect. The programme evinced considerable taste, consisting of an admirably arranged selection of songs and glees, from the works of popular composers, and which were executed in good style, several of them being loudly *encored*. Horne's beautiful duett, I know a Bank, was given by Miss Bentley and Mr Griffiths with pleasing effect, and was loudly applauded. Miss Bentley sang The Soldier's Wife, and Home, Sweet Home, with touching sweetness, meeting with an enthusiastic *redemande* in each case, and in the latter instance substituted, with equal effect, the well known ballad, Comin' through the Rye. Miss Heath gave the pathetic song from La

Sonnambula, The Spell is Broken, receiving a deserved *encore,* and substituting, I canna' mind my Wheel. Mr Polgrean gave, Let me like a Soldier fall, and, My Fatherland, being *encored* on each occasion, when he substituted for the former Braham's fine old song, The Bay of Biscay, and for the latter, Goodbye, Sweetheart. He also gave, by desire, The Country Fair, with ventriloquial illustrations, eliciting the most uproarious laughter.

At the conclusion, a vote of thanks was passed to the singers for their services, which was suitably acknowledged by Mr T. L. Emery. The proceeds of the meeting and concert are to be devoted towards extending the library connected with the institution.

The various events in the early days of the association took place at Hartshill School. From the very beginning Colin Minton Campbell had expressed the view that the association really needed a home of its own and, in spite of the setbacks, he went ahead and paid for the construction of a separate building – originally known as "The Hartshill Working Men's Institution" – next to the Minton Cottages on what is now Hartshill Road. Four extra cottages were also built adjoining the new hall. The Minton Cottages, like Hartshill Church, had been designed by George Gilbert Scott but, the local papers reported, Campbell apparently commissioned a local architect, "Mr Edgar of Stoke", to design the new buildings.

Steve Birks, who runs the Stoke-on-Trent local history website thepotteries.org, has drawn my attention to another website (http://www.uea.ac.uk/~t009/ArtistBiography.htm) which contains a brief biography of an architect called Robert Edgar (c. 1837-73) who is described as "a London-based architect who studied under Sir George Gilbert Scott (1811-78) and was probably influenced by Scott's neo-Gothic style" and whose works include Compton School in Leek (1863) and the Wedgwood Institute in Burslem (1869). Both the local links and the fact that he was a pupil of Scott suggest that this was "Mr Edgar of Stoke".

The newspaper reports also credit Mr Sutton of Newcastle with executing the brickwork and Mr Young of Lincoln the stone and timber work.

Building work began in October 1858 and was completed at the end of the year ready for it to be opened by a series of inaugural events in January 1859 which were prominently advertised on the front pages of *The Staffordshire Sentinel* and *The Staffordshire Advertiser* in their issues of 1st and 8th January (see opposite page) coupled with editorial mentions on the inside pages drawing attention to the advertisement. The events themselves were reported at length in both papers.

The articles began by looking back on the formation of the Working Men's Association three years earlier, the reverse it suffered "from some cause or another" following the death of Herbert Minton and its resuscitation by

HARTSHILL WORKINGMEN'S INSTITUTION, INAUGURAL ENTERTAINMENT.

THE Committee have much pleasure in announcing to the Members and the Public, that the NEW BUILDING of the above INSTITUTION, will be OPENED ON MONDAY, the 10th January, 1839, on which occasion the INAUGURAL ADDRESS WILL BE DELIVERED BY THE REV. W. D. ISAAC, to be followed by Addresses from the REV. ERSKINE CLARKE, of St. Michael's, Derby ; the REV. L. T. STAMER, Rector of Stoke; and others of the Gentry and Clergy. The Admission, on this Evening, to the BODY OF THE HALL will be by Ticket, FREE ; to be obtained from the SECRETARY and the COMMITTEE ; a few Reserve Tickets for the GALLERY, ONE SHILLING EACH, to be had from the SECRETARY only.

A CONVERSAZIONE will he be held on WEDNESDAY EVENING, the 12th January, 1859, when there will be an EXHIBITION OF PAINTINGS, POTTERY, CHOICE PRINTS, ILLUSTRATED WORKS, &c., lent by gentlemen of the district. ESSAYS on interesting topics will be read, and a SELECTION OF INSTRUMENTAL MUSIC will be Performed, Mr. JOHN EMERY, Jun., presiding at the Pianoforte.

Coffee will he served at Eight o'clock : Doors open at Half-past Six — ADMISSION — ONE SHILLING. The Exhibition will be open the Public on Thursday, the 13th of January, — Admission, From Twelve to Four, One Shilling ; from Six to Ten o'clock, Sixpence Each.

On SATURDAY, the 15th instant, the HALL will be OPENED at Two o'clock p.m. There will be, an EXHIBITION OF PAINTINGS and PRINTS lent for the occasion, and in the Centre of the Hall will be placed an "ILLUMINATED TREE" on which a variety of Useful Articles will be offered for Sale; the Proceeds to be applied to the Library. THE SECRETARY will most thankfully receive Donations for this object. The HARTSHILL BAND will be in Attendance. Admission, from Two to Four o'clock, SIXPENCE EACH ; and from Four to Eight THREEPENCE EACH.

On TUESDAY EVENING, the 18th instant, the Entertainments will be brought to a close by a TEA PARTY. Tea on the Table at Six o'clock. ADDRESSES WILL BE DELIVERED by the REV. W. D. ISAAC ; the REV. W. L. ROSENTHALL of Willenhall ; and other Gentlemen, and a SELECTION OF MUSIC PERFORMED. Tickets ONE SHILLING EACH, to be obtained from the HON. SECRETARY and COMMITTEE.

R. LEASON, HON. SEC.

Hartshill, Stoke-upon-Trent, Dec. 30th, 1858.

The above is a reconstruction of the four column inches advertisement which appeared on the front page of The Staffordshire Sentinel and Midland Counties Advertiser of 1st and 8th January 1858. The column width is virtually the same as in 1859, but in the interests of legibility the size of the type and the line spacing has been increased slightly.

A similar advertisement was published in The Staffordshire Advertiser on the same dates.

Colin Minton Campbell leading to, in the words of the *Sentinel*:

> The idea - spontaneous and unsolicited - in Mr Campbell's mind of crowning his numerous kindnesses to the association, by an act of munificence and practical generosity, which will ever endear his name to those who take the same warm interest in the labouring classes as himself, and also of the members of those classes themselves who will have an opportunity of participating in the result of his benevolence, by erecting, at his own cost, a building suitable for the purposes of the association, and presenting it to them, a free gift.

Both articles then described the building inside and out in great detail, although they disagreed on the dimensions of the "reading-room or lecture-hall". "About 46 feet by 23 feet" according to *The Advertiser* but slightly less – "40 ft by 20 ft" – in the *Sentinel*'s report. To avoid quibbling about a few inches more or less on each dimension let's take *The Advertiser*'s figures as the more accurate.

The opening meeting was well attended by "those for whose special benefit the edifice has been raised" and the interest they took in the proceedings appeared to augur well for the future success of the institution. Colin Minton Campbell presided and he was accompanied on the platform by "the Revds. W. D. Isaac, L. T. Stamer, J. Erskine Clarke, of Derby, H. Gough and J. H. Macaulay; F. Bishop Esq., and J. Samuda Esq. In the gallery were a number of ladies and the Rev. H. S. Wood, P. Walker and W. H. Jackson; M. F. Blakiston Esq., R. Steele Esq., &c., &c."

The proceedings commenced with the singing of the hymn, "Glory be to God on high," followed by a prayer read by the Rev. W. D. Isaac composed specially for the occasion. Then the Chairman, C. M. Campbell, reflected on the history of the association and his hopes for the future:

> You know what we did with the old reading room. We had all the best papers of the day and week, and most of the best periodicals. We also commenced getting up a library, which, like all other things, must have a beginning, which in this case was not a great one; but I now hope that before long we shall have a large collection of the most useful and interesting works of the day. We also commenced a class for the working men, but unfortunately it did not last - the fault of which, I think, was that we commenced our class too soon. Our men were driven out by the boys of the parish, who came in such numbers that the men had no room, and retired, I suppose, in disgust. I may here say here that these classes are not for the boys of the parish, but for the elder persons; and I think we should all do what we can to revive the classes and induce the older people of the place to attend them. Then another feature of the institution will be the periodical delivery of lectures of an interesting and attractive kind, and musical entertainments perhaps similar to those at Stoke.

This was followed by addresses by the Rev. W. D. Isaac, Rev. L. T. Stamer and Rev. J. Erskine Clarke, the latter speaking for more than twice as long as the other two clergymen together in what was described by the *Sentinel* as "a lengthy and very eloquent speech". Erskine Clarke talked about his dislike of the term "Institution" (he preferred "Association"), the importance of reading newspapers and books, the value of the lectures and classes planned for the hall, the dangers of drink, his experience with savings banks and his hope that the committee of the institution would establish a penny bank. He concluded by saying that "he hoped that the institution would go on and prosper, and flourish more and more in the highest purposes".

The *Advertiser* report contained one sentence which – interestingly but not surprisingly – did not appear in the *Sentinel*. It said: "That man surely ought to be ashamed of himself who felt so little interest in his country as not to read his newspaper – be it the *Staffordshire Advertiser* or whatever it might be – once a week."

One point referred to in Mr Clarke's speech which was reported by both papers referred to the prophecy by some unnamed authority of the day that in fifty years' time – i.e. by the early twentieth century – the only books that would be available would be in the form of newspapers. As that hasn't happened, one wonders how much truth there is in recent comments such as: "The era of the traditional newspaper could soon be over as scientists launch production of a revolutionary electronic version - made out of plastic." (*Daily Mail*, 15th October 2008).

But back to January 1859. An illuminated address (see page 18) was presented to Colin Minton Campbell, who expressed his gratitude and said that, "if what should be done in that room, should only come up to one half of his expectations, he should be quite satisfied." After the association's treasurer, Mr Samuda, had proposed a vote of thanks to Mr Campbell and the speakers, Mr Clarke "responded in a humorous and clever speech" and the opening ceremony concluded with the singing of the National Anthem by the entire company led by the choir of Hartshill Church.

There was a flurry of activities in the first week of the institution's existence: not only the opening ceremony itself but also exhibitions and musical entertainment concluding with an evening tea party and concert. The latter, unfortunately, did not go absolutely smoothly as the following extract from the report in *The Staffordshire Advertiser* shows:

> There was a large attendance, the room being completely filled. The company having partaken of an excellent tea, the chair was taken by Mr. Campbell, who stated that the Rev. W. D. Isaac had been expected to preside, but that that afternoon be had sent a note to the committee stating that having

To Colin Minton Campbell, Esq.

We the undersigned, being the Committee of the Hartshill Working Men's Institution, take this opportunity of congratulating you on the opening of this building, so beautiful in its architectural features, and so well adapted for the purposes it was designed to promote. As the spontaneous creation of your liberal and enlightened spirit, we earnestly hope that your aspirations for the public good, in connection with this institution, may be most fully realised, and that the building may long endure as a memorial of your patriotic feeling, and a monitor to your wealthy neighbours to 'go and do likewise.'

In the name of the inhabitants generally, we offer you our most hearty thanks, and with our most sincere wishes for the health, happiness, and prosperity of yourself, and family,

We subscribe ourselves, sir.

Your faithful servants,

This is a reconstruction of the illuminated address presented to Colin Minton Campbell. We have no way of knowing what it actually looked like, apart from the fact that it was "was beautifully written and illuminated on vellum by Mr Underwood, of Birmingham" and signed by the Rev. W. D. Isaac, Chairman, and the members of the committee.

heard that songs were to be introduced, he could not conscientiously take any part in the proceedings. Mr. Campbell took strong exception to the course pursued by the reverend gentleman in keeping the committee in ignorance of his intention until the last moment, or rather giving them to understand that he would attend, and then failing them at the eleventh hour. Having made this explanation, which he thought was due to the parish, Mr. Campbell said they must all feel exceedingly gratified with the result of the opening entertainment, for up to that time, exclusive of the tea party, £20. 10s. had been realised for the benefit of the institution, which was a respectable sum with which to commence the formation of a library. He hoped the classes would he opened in the course of the week, and the committee were determined to succeed.

Mr Isaac may have declined to take part, but there was a talk by Rev. W. L. Rosenthal of Willenhall and the Rev. H. Gough of Penkhull pronounced the Benediction with the performance a number of musical items between the two.

For the first year or so after the opening of the institution things seemed to go well. A library of 300 volumes had been built up. There were 121 members with an average of eleven attending each night. However, the beerhouses were still proving to be a greater attraction for the working men of the area. As a result the institution was closed down and reopened on several occasions. A musical evening for example was held in March 1869 but it was reported that the attendance "was not very large". By 1871 the building was being referred to as a "Public Hall" and advertised to let "for any kind of function at moderate fees".

Although the *Sentinel* report of the opening ceremony referred to the building being a "free gift" it would appear that Colin Minton Campbell initially remained the owner for, according to the conveyance document drawn up when The Newcastle Players bought the property in 1969, in March 1863 he sold it or transferred the ownership of it to Robert Minton Taylor, who was later to be his partner in the Minton Brick and Tile Co, and Thomas William Minton.

Local historian Richard Talbot has provided me with information from an 1891 issue of the *Stoke-on-Trent Parish Magazine* in his archives referring to Thomas Minton and Herbert Minton-Senhouse as the owners, for they had written to the Church saying that they were prepared to hand the Institute over to trustees to be elected by the inhabitants of Hartshill and the June 1891 issue of the magazine confirmed that they did this:

THE INSTITUTE. — In accordance with the wish of Mr. T. Minton and Mr. H. Minton-Senhouse, the owners of the Institute, a meeting of householders was called on Friday, May 22nd, to nominate trustees, to whom the building may be transferred for the use of the village. The trustees nominated were, Mr. T. Minton, Mr. H. Minton-Senhouse, The Vicar, Mr. Knight, Mr. Clive, Mr. Phillips, Mr. Henshall, Mr. Orme, Mr. Udall.

To them the present owners have most kindly promised to convey the property: and thus, through their generosity, the purpose for which the building was originally designed by Mr. Campbell, will be strictly carried out.

At the same meeting, a committee was elected to co-operate with the trustees in the management of the room.

It was from about this time that the building became known as The Institute, although the former name of The Institution still occurs in some reports.

However, in spite of all this, the actual ownership of the building must have remained with the Minton family until much later. Although the 1969 conveyance refers to the transfer of ownership from Colin Minton Campbell to Robert Minton Taylor and Thomas William Minton in 1863, there is no mention of when Herbert Minton-Senhouse became involved, but the document does record that his widow, Ann Darby Minton Senhouse, sold or donated the building to "The Lichfield Diocesan Trust and the then Vicar [Rev. Bertram Liddle Hope] and Churchwardens of the Parish of Hartshill" on 7th December 1923. By that time it had long been in use by the Church, although I am not sure when the name changed from "The Institute" to "The Hartshill Church Institute".

Vol. 12. SEPTEMBER, 1903. No. 9.

HARTSHILL & BASFORD
(STAFFS.)
PARISH MAGAZINE.

HARTSHILL.

Vicar: REV. A. M. FOSBROOKE, M.A., THE VICARAGE.
Assistant Curate: REV. H. D. LYON, 1 QUEEN'S ROAD.
Commissioned Lay Readers: MR J. HAMLET, HARTSHILL. MR T. E. D. RICKERBY, MINTONS BUILDINGS.
Churchwardens: MR T. B. UDALL, MR G. E. PHILLIMORE.

Public Services.

Hartshill Church.

Holy Communion, all Sundays at 8 a.m.; also on 1st and 3rd Sundays at Noon; 4th Sunday, 7 a.m.; Holy Days and Thursdays at 7-30 a.m.

Mattins, on Sundays, 11 a.m., with Sermon. Holy Days and Fridays, 10-30 a.m. All other days, 8-30 a.m.

Evensong, on Sundays 6-30 p.m., and on Wednesdays 7-30 p.m., with Sermon. Other Days at 5-30 p.m.

Parish Clerk: MR S. BARLOW, Longfield Place.

S. Matthew's, Kingscroft.

Holy Communion, First and Third Sunday in each Month at 8 a.m.

Evensong, with Sermon, Sundays, 6-30 p.m., and on Thursdays, 7-45 p.m., with Address.

Wardens, MR W. AUSTIN, MR THORNBURY.

For Sittings at the Parish Church application should be made to either Warden, or to Mr S. Barlow, Parish Clerk.

BASFORD.

Priest-in-Charge: REV. CHARLES P. WAY, M.A., 10 Lord Street, Basford.
Wardens: MR R. E. CLARK, MR C. E. WALKER.

Public Services.

Holy Communion, Every Sunday at 8 a.m., and on the First Sunday of the Month at Noon also.

Mattins, on Sundays, 11 a.m., with Sermon. Daily, 11 a.m.

Evensong, on Sundays, 6-30 p.m., and on Wednesdays, 7-30 p.m., with Sermon. Daily, 7-30. ALL SEATS at S. Mark's are FREE and unappropriated. The Church is open daily from 10 a.m. to 8 p.m.

PRICE ONE PENNY.—To be had from the Clergy, and District Visitors of the Parish; also from Vyse & Hill, Wolfe Street, Stoke-on-Trent.

PRINTED BY C. H. VYSE, CHURCH STREET, STOKE-ON-TRENT

The front cover of an early issue of the HARTSHILL & BASFORD (STAFFS) PARISH MAGAZINE held in the Minton Centre in Hartshill.

5. The Hartshill Church Institute – The Early Years

Hartshill Church was originally a daughter church of St. Peter's Church, Stoke but at some time in the nineteenth century it became a parish in its own right. Nevertheless, as mentioned in the previous chapter, items about the Hartshill Institute were still appearing in the *Stoke-on-Trent Parish Magazine* in the early 1890s even though Hartshill Church probably had its own magazine by then. Unfortunately records for the last decade of the nineteenth century and first thirty years or so of the twentieth century are thin on the ground. We have no indication when the words "Working Men" disappeared from the hall's title or when it became officially known as The Hartshill Church Institute.

A few copies of the *HARTSHILL & BASFORD PARISH MAGAZINE* are held in the Minton Centre (see previous page) but they contain little useful information about the Institute. In the September 1903 issue for example it was reported that the Band of Hope would re-open that month but without any indication of where. It also said that the Social Club's Winter Session would open on Tuesday, 15th September, at 7-30 p.m. with an open Social Evening and Smoking Concert. A Sub-Committee was arranging a musical programme, and the Vicar was "looking for a suitable man to give a short address". The item went on to say that men of all classes would be warmly welcomed, admission would be free and the organisers were hoping to see a full room. There was no mention of the Institute in either case, but possibly that was where the events took place.

1903 was long before Hartshill Parish Church Entertainers (see page 33) were founded, but if they had been in existence they would no doubt have been interested in the advertisement opposite from the September 1903 issue of the parish magazine.

There are no more magazines archived in the Minton Centre until 1917 when it was announced that:

> a Wolf Cub Pack is now connected with our troop of Scouts, and particulars can be obtained from the Scoutmaster.

No doubt the Pack met in the Institute since the cover of the December 1920 issue of the magazine lists:

LOVELY PRESENTATION ARTICLES—

Purses	Inkstands
Satchells	Work Boxes
Chatelaines	Glove Boxes
Music Cases	Handkerchief Boxes
Albums	Photo Frames
Needle Cases	Writing Cases

TOILET REQUIREMENTS of every kind—

Hair Brushes	Fringe Nets
Tooth Brushes	Zephyr Fringes
Dressing Combs	Spray Bottles
Fancy Combs	Pearl Necklets
Perfumery	Oriental Beads
Hinde's Specialities	Crystal Pins

AMATEUR THEATRICALS—

Grease Paints	Eyebrow Pencils
Lining Pencils	Papier Poudrè
Rouges (various)	Spirit Gum
Tinted Face Powders	Crepe Hair
Cocoa Butter	Beards

100 Character or other Wigs for Selection on Hire.

F. W. DALE,
Fancy and Toilet Goods Dealer,
Stafford Street,
HANLEY.

A 1903 advertisement from the HARTSHILL & BASFORD (STAFFS) PARISH MAGAZINE aimed at, amongst others, "AMATEUR THEATRICALS", but about fifty years too early for the Hartshill Parish Church Entertainers (see page 33).

Boy Scouts – Wednesday and Thursday in Institute, 7-30 p.m.

The list also contains:

Bible Class for Youths – Sunday, in Institute, 2-30 p.m.

Girls, however, had their Sunday bible class in the schoolroom, as did the Sunday School teachers on the first Monday in the month and the G.F.S. on Tuesday evenings, while other meetings were held at St. Matthew's and in the Vicarage.

The Parish Magazines for the couple of years prior to the appointment of the Reverend Reginald H Wyatt (see Chapter 6) give some clue to the church activities that went on the Institute.

In 1930 these included:

- Whist Drives to raise money for the Missions to Seamen, parochial funds and the Sale of Work Funds. Tickets for the first of these cost 1/6 each, including refreshments, and for the other two 1/-.
- A Pantomime presented by the Scouts, half the proceeds being devoted to the Institute Funds and the other half to the Scouts' own Camp Funds.
- A talk by Sadhu Christananda. The Parish Magazine commented that it would be "very interesting to see a real Indian, and to hear what he has got to say about his country, and about Missions to non-Christians."
- An Entertainment by the members of the Girls Friendly Society in March 1930 and a dance organised by the G.F.S., the proceeds from both events going to G.F.S. Funds.
- A meeting addressed by Mrs Collier of the South African Church Railway Mission.
- Mr Farrell's Sunday Afternoon Class, which "Any lad may join on presenting himself at that time", met each Sunday afternoon at 2-30 and in November they held their first social for which there "was quite a room-full of members and friends, and they had a right good time".

And in 1931:
- A concert by the Sparklets' Concert Party, the proceeds going towards the equipment of the Guides' Stall in the Sale of Work.
- A Rummage Sale with the proceeds going towards the Refreshment Stall.
- A Tea and Entertainment on Shrove Tuesday: "There were not many vacant places at tea, and quite a number came in afterwards. A thoroughly enjoyable evening was spent."
- Whist Drives organised by various bodies within the Church.

John and Lulu Barstow photographed at the Newcastle Players' 40th Anniversary celebrations in January 1975. Their wedding reception on Christmas Eve 1927 was held in the Institute.

Photograph by Paul Tunstill

- The Scouts' Annual Entertainment, the magazine commenting that "the lads acquitted themselves well, before good audiences". It also reported that the newly-formed troop in connection with the Parish Church was going strong and met each Tuesday in the Schools and each Thursday in the Institute.

We know too that the hall was let out for private functions – and that information came from a Newcastle Players source. On Saturday, 24th December 1927 it was the venue for the wedding reception of John and Lulu Barstow, later to be members of the society. In fact John was Secretary from 1940 to 1952, Vice-President from 1952 to 1963 and President from 1963 until his death at the age of 77 in 1977. It was John's nostalgia for the hall in which he and Lulu had started their married life that led him to investigate why it was apparently standing empty and unused in the late 1960s.

But that is jumping too far ahead and must wait for a later chapter. First we must look at the busiest period in the Institute's history: the Wyatt Years.

6. The Wyatt Years – 1931 to 1960

While researching the history of The Hartshill Church Institute I have been in contact with a lot of people who grew up in Hartshill in the thirties, forties and fifties of the twentieth century. This was the period during which The Reverend R H Wyatt was Vicar and, as one of my correspondents wrote, "the Vicar (Mr Wyatt) made good use of the Institute". Reginald H Wyatt in fact took up his office as Vicar of Holy Trinity Church, Hartshill towards the end of 1931 and retired 29 years later, the last services at which he officiated as Vicar being on Easter Sunday 1960. He was the longest-serving Vicar in the Church's history.

People's memories of the hall and the activities that went on there were vivid, but – as is so often the case with memories that are not backed up by documentary evidence – not necessarily completely accurate. For example, one lady was insistent that the Vicar would only play Victor Silvester* records at the Saturday night dances, nothing else. Others disagreed with this and they were obviously right, as you will see later in this chapter. Fortunately the years during which Mr Wyatt was Vicar are quite well documented, which is possibly a testimony to his good stewardship.

Significantly there is almost a complete set of parish magazines for that period held in the Minton Centre in Hartshill and they have been a useful source of documented evidence. Unfortunately there are no magazines at the centre for the period from 1940 to 1946. It was of course wartime but the magazine was still being published, albeit not so frequently as is borne out by a question raised at the January 1942 meeting of the Parochial Church Council by Mr Wright who wanted to know if it was absolutely necessary for the magazine to be issued quarterly and not monthly as before. The Vicar said that it was a measure of national economy, and also due to the lack of advertisers. Local businesses had nothing to sell, so they had withdrawn their advertisements which presumably provided the financial backing for the magazine.

---

*Victor Silvester was a champion ballroom dancer who formed an orchestra in 1935 to provide purely instrumental, strict tempo music for ballroom dancing. His records sold 75 million copies and he remained popular with ballroom dancers for something like forty years.

The Reverend Reginald H. Wyatt in October 1931.
Photograph by courtesy of Holy Trinity Church, Hartshill

Another source – again not complete, but overlapping other sources – is the minutes of the Parochial Church Council. The current secretary, Angela Mountford, has the minutes of the Church Annual General Meetings covering the period from 1936 to 1969 and beyond. Unfortunately the minutes of the Parochial Church Council itself have not fared so well. The Staffordshire Record Office in Stafford holds the minutes for the period from 1931 to 1960 but the minutes for the final few years of the Church's ownership of the Institute have disappeared without trace. Presumably they were disposed of because somebody thought they were no longer of any interest to anybody.

Nevertheless, in spite of gaps in one record or another, the documents I have been able to consult have provided me with written confirmation and clarification of much of the anecdotal evidence I obtained about the hall's use as The Hartshill Church Institute.

Different people remember different activities but many mentioned the Saturday night dances, the Youth Club and the shows put on by the Hartshill Entertainers, not forgetting the Brownies and Guides. But there were others too and not all of them were activities connected with or organised by the church. It seems to me that the only logical way to chronicle what went on during the Wyatt Years is to discuss the church's activities at least in alphabetical order – if for no other reason than to avoid being accused of giving one preference over another.

Anniversary Missed

It may seem strange to start with something that did not take place in the Institute, but I can think of nowhere else to mention it.

On Saturday, 10th January 1959 the building was 100 years old but the centenary seems to have passed unnoticed. The 150th Anniversary did not suffer a similar fate (see page 108).

Annual General Meeting

The Church's Annual General Meeting or Annual Parochial Church Meeting was held in the Institute from 1936 and continued to be held there throughout the Wyatt years. In 1938 the Vicar commented that the meetings were open to all residents of Hartshill "be they Roman, Nonconformist or Anglican" and said that he hoped for a record attendance, adding: "It is your right to know how financial matters stand relating to the Church, and how the money is spent, and so if you have any complaint or grievance, don't nurse it – or stay away – come along and ventilate it. We welcome candid criticisms as well as helpful suggestions."

Beetle Drive

In the forties – and later – Beetle Drives and Whist Drives were popular events in church halls around the country. The latter featured prominently on the Institute's programme of events (see later in this chapter), but I have only been able to find one reference to a Beetle Drive. This took place on Monday, 24th April, 1944.

Brownies

Although the Girl Guides are listed on the cover of the January 1930 parish magazine as meeting in the Institute on Wednesday evenings, I found no reference to the Brownies in any of the documents I was able to consult until 1948 when there was an appeal in the parish magazine for girls from the ages of 4 to 7 years to fill the gap caused by the older Brownies passing on into the Girl Guides. When Miss Edna Candlin resigned as Brown Owl in 1958, it was said that she had held office in the Pack for over fourteen years, in other words since at least 1944. However, several ladies I have talked to remember being in the Brownies in the thirties, so Miss Candlin would not have been the first Brown Owl.

At one time the Pack, the 8th Hartshill Brownies, met at the Institute on Tuesday evenings at 6-30 p.m. but this changed later to Wednesday, starting at 6-00 p.m.

In 1957 it was reported that the Brownies were getting along quite happily and they had no worries, but the Guide Captain was leaving the district and, if she could not be replaced, the Company would have to close and, without a Guide Company, the Brownie Pack would be of very little use.

The problem must have been overcome, because three years later it was reported that both the Guides and Brownies were doing extremely well. There was a waiting list and a second Pack had been formed. In fact the Guides and Brownies appear to have continued to use the Institute for their meetings until well into the sixties.

C.E.M.S.

The Church of England Men's Society normally met in other premises within the parish, but on Thursday, 11th December 1958 it met in the Institute, as its regular meeting place, St. Matthew's Hall, was booked for the Old Peoples' Christmas Party. The guest speaker was Mr. Eric Lever, City Probation Officer, who gave a report on the C.E.M.S. Conference held recently at Southampton. Members of Basford branch of the C.E.M.S. also attended.

Concerts

The Institute had a small stage at the end opposite the gallery. In 1937 the PCC approved the expenditure of £4.10.0. on an extension to the stage, but when the Newcastle Players acquired the hall thirty years later it was still not very big. Nevertheless quite a lot of concerts were presented on it during the thirties and forties organised by the Choir, Guides and Rangers, Scouts and the Sunday School. A concert was also usually part of the programme at the Annual Harvest Tea. These events featured both home-grown talent and imported performers such as the Sparklets Concert Party and the Tunstall Youth Concert Party. Admission prices ranged from sixpence in 1932 to 1/6 in 1949. This looks quite an increase but, to be fair, tickets for the Choir concert in 1932 were one shilling and parishioners were urged to buy a ticket to encourage choir members even if they couldn't go to the concert.

The content of the concerts varied, as did the size of the audiences. Some reports were encouraging, referring to the hall being "well filled with an enthusiastic audience who much enjoyed the various songs, dual monologues, sketches and community singing". However, another commented that a splendid programme at Scouts Annual Concert had been heartily enjoyed by the audience but it was composed very largely of Scouts' parents and friends and, "although this is the kind of audience we most appreciate, the Institute Funds would have benefited to a greater extent if church people generally had been willing to give their support."

It would appear that in the fifties the style of the concerts changed with the formation of the Hartshill Parish Church Entertainers (see page 33).

Dances

Dances were held in the Institute from at least the early thirties. They were run by various organisations such as the Girls Friendly Society, the Choir and so on. Dancing was also a feature of the annual Harvest Tea and Social Evenings. In 1932 the parish magazine contained the following comment on "a very pleasant event . . . in the Church Institute on Thursday, 26th May, 1932":

> The Institute was tastefully decorated with suspended paper streamers, which had been put up specially for the occasion. A gramophone and portable wireless set (loaned by Mr Ridgway and Mr Chatfield, respectively) provided some of the music for dancing.

In these days of powerful amplification it is difficult to imagine how "a gramophone and portable wireless set" could provide enough volume for several dozen dancers. This was less likely to have been a problem at an event in 1934 referred to as "The Queen's Effort" organised by "Miss Jackson (presumably the Hartshill Queen of the time) and her family". The Institute, which was "laid out as a tea lounge", "looked charming; never have we seen the room more cosy and inviting". The music on this occasion was supplied by Phil Botham and his Melody Makers.

During the summer of 1935 the PCC decided that the Institute floor had become unsuitable for dances and they were suspended for a time. They resumed in the autumn when the parish magazine reported: "A new floor has been laid for the benefit of the dancing community, whom we trust will appreciate and use the same on every possible occasion".

In 1936 a Carnival Dance was held in the Institute on Thursday, 16th April, "which proved a very jolly social event".

However, what people, who were in their teens or twenties in the years following World War II, remember in particular are the Saturday night dances organised initially by the Vicar. These appear to have started in 1948 when the parish magazine contained the following two announcements:

Young People Please Note

that the Saturday evening DANCES will commence again on Saturday, 18th September, at 7-30 p.m. in the Institute. We want a good crowd that night, so tell all your pals to come along.

Old Time Dances.

It has been decided to hold OLD TIME DANCES once a fortnight, commencing on Thursday, 16th September, at 7-30 p.m. The few old Time Dances held have been very enjoyable, and we look forward to many more of them in the future.

Come and enjoy an evening's programme of dance music played by Harry Davidson and his band. Admission 1/-.

It is, of course, highly unlikely that Harry Davidson and his band were there in person. They broadcast regularly on such BBC programmes as *Music While You Work* and the old time dance music programme *Those Were The Days*. I assume that the Vicar was playing records by Davidson and his band. In fact, one person who contacted me with memories referred to him as "the first DJ in The Potteries". But he did more than that according to another correspondent who wrote:

The Vicar put on the records, sold pop and crisps during the interval and generally kept an eye on us all! Some of the boys in their late teens had started to buy records and asked to have them played so we got all the latest releases, but it was frowned on when we started to jitterbug!!

The weekly dances really got under way in 1950 when the Hartshill Drill Hall closed down its dancing on Saturday nights. The Vicar felt that the Church should cater for its own youth but, he wrote in the magazine, "it is useless unless she has the co-operation and support of the young people themselves. If they really need a weekly Dance and intend to support it wholeheartedly, then the Church will meet the need."

It would appear that the dances did not get off to an altogether good start, as the following items appeared the following year in the magazine:

Dances in the Institute

It has been decided to resume the Dances on Saturday nights in the Institute, and instead of the old recorded music the "Jacdon Trio" band has been engaged to play for the season. The first Dance will be held on Saturday, 6th October, 7-30 to 10-15 p.m., when we hope all the young people of the parish will come along. The admission will be the modest sum of 1/- and dancers can be assured of a good evening's dancing. Make it known among your friends.

A Reminder to all Dancers

It has been decided to start again the Dances on Saturday nights in the institute, commencing on Saturday, 6th October, at 7-30 p.m. The music will be supplied by the "Jacdon Trio" band and not by the recorded music as hitherto. Whether the dances will continue depends upon the support received from our young people.

The charge for admission will be the modest sum of 1/-. Where else can one get an evening's dancing for such a small sum?

As a musician myself I am intrigued to know who the Jacdon Trio were and what instruments they played. Unfortunately my enquiries have not come up with any answers.

Be that as it may, this time things progressed much better. In 1953 it was reported that the Saturday night dances were going very well and all seemed to be enjoying themselves. The dances also made a contribution the cost of running the Institute.

Some people have memories of skiffle groups playing at the Institute, presumably in the interval when the band took a break.

Brian Yelland remembers going to the Saturday dances between 1953 and 1955. He went on to become a professional entertainer, compère and cabaret artist, performing, as Brian Delmar, all over the world, but his first public appearance on stage was at the Institute when he played the guitar and sang songs during the interval in the dancing.

Regrettably by early 1958 the Saturday evening dance club had ceased to function and the Institute had lost its main source of income.

Brian Yelland, whose first public performance was on the Institute stage, seen here (right) in the mid 1950s with his first group, the group's manager (second right) and two young lady admirers.

Photograph supplied by Brian Yelland

The Entertainers

At the 1950 Annual General Meeting the Vicar reported that the social activities of the Church had been the same as usual and included, the minutes record, "such organisations as Girl Guides, Brownies, Scouts, Cubs, St. John's (sic) Ambulance Brigade, Mothers Union and now a new organization – the Hartshill Parish Church Entertainers. This, said the Vicar, was something which had been needed for many years to provide amusement for our own people and under the guidance of Mr. E. Evans they were doing very well indeed and he considered it to be a very valuable acquisition to the social life of the parish."

Edgar Evans, who owned a cycle shop in Hartshill Road opposite what is now the Britannia Building Society branch, was the Sunday School Superintendent and had been heavily involved in the various concerts at the Institute during the thirties and forties. He and his wife Connie (née Hobson)

33

```
HARTSHILL PARISH CHURCH
ENTERTAINERS.

The members will present three Sketches :
"OUT OF THE FRYING PAN"
"THREE BLIND MICE"
"GENERALLY USEFUL"
                (by permission of the Publishers,
                    Abel Heywood & Sons Ltd)

on December 1st and 3rd, 1949.
at 7-30 p.m. in the Institute. Tickets 1/- each.
```

Reproduction of an advertisement from the Parish Magazine for the first performance by the Hartshill Parish Church Entertainers.

married late in life and were the driving force behind The Entertainers.

The Vicar's remarks at the AGM suggest that The Entertainers had been formed in 1949 and the first reference to the group that I have found relates to three sketches performed in the Institute on December 1st and 3rd, 1949 (see above). Yet, at the PCC meeting a month earlier it was reported that "an amount of £5 had been received from Mr. E. Evans on behalf of the Hartshill Parish Church Entertainers".

Be that as it may, The Entertainers got off to a good start and attracted good audiences. In 1950 they performed an evening of three short plays on two nights in April, held a successful jumble sale and were hoping to return to the stage again in November or December. In fact they had to wait until February 1951. Their performance was reported at length in the Parish Magazine:

> Once again the entertainers gave of their best in the two plays entitled "Sam's Daughter" and "Bye Baby Bunting" which they gave to packed houses recently. After overcoming many difficulties *(i.e.,* sickness, change in the cast and suitable nights to meet the wishes of all members), the entertainers did remarkably well in their respective parts and well deserved the applause of their parts and well deserved the applause of their visitors and friends. Mr. E. Evans was responsible for the production of the plays as well as stage manager, etc., and we congratulate him upon the success of the show. The whole cast were on their toes all the time and put plenty of life in their parts without over

A picture of the Hartshill Parish Church Entertainers which appeared in the booklet published by Hartshill Parish Church to mark its 150th Anniversary in 1992. Edgar Evans is standing on the right of the back row.

doing it. Miss Brunt played popular pieces on the piano between the plays which added to the evening's enjoyment. The entertainers were responsible also for the Shrove Tuesday's Social, and provided a very enjoyable and varied programme. It was quite a family party with plenty of games and fun for all ages.

Over the next few years The Entertainers suffered mixed fortunes. They presented Passion Plays at Easter over a period of several years but as the decade progressed they were faced with a series of obstacles: falling audience numbers, tighter official regulations governing public performances, falling membership, illness and lack of success in recruiting new members. At the 1957 AGM Mr Evans commented on the poor support for The Entertainers from parishioners, adding that if better support of their efforts was not forthcoming there was a possibility they would lose the services of the young people.

In spite of these difficulties though The Entertainers raised regular amounts for church funds and in 1958, when new oil heating apparatus was

Plays performed
by
The Hartshill Church Entertainers

1949 – Thursday and Saturday, 1st and 3rd December:

Out of the Frying Pan
Three Blind Mice
Generally Useful

1950 – Thursday and Saturday, 11th and 13th April:

Difficult to Please
The Silent Woman
The Stroke of Twelve

1951 – Thursday and Saturday, 1st and 3rd of February:

Sam's Daughter
Bye Baby Bunting

1952 – Thursday, 31st January and Saturday, 2nd February:

Rejuvenation by Jessie S. Mayo
Wanted a Wife by Ralph Parr

1953 – Thursday and Saturday, 3rd and 5th December:

Pearly Pearls

1956 – December (exact date not known):

The Shirt

The only plays where the author's name is known are the two performed in 1952. The six in 1949 and 1950 were presented "by permission of the publishers, Abel Heywood & Sons Ltd." I have only been able to trace the titles of two of the Passion Plays. They were *Before the Dawn* in 1953 and *Victory of the Cross* in 1957.

installed in the Church at a cost of approximately £303, which included the first delivery of oil fuel, The Entertainers were among the organisations that contributed sums of money.

To us, The Newcastle Players, who have performed for the past fifty years at the Mitchell Memorial Theatre on a stage with an acting area approximately 28 by 17 feet plus wing space and an apron in front, it is difficult to understand how it was possible to put on plays on such a small stage as the one in the Institute with no wings and no apron. But the Entertainers did.

Girls Friendly Society

Like the C.E.M.S. referred to on page 29, the G.F.S. also met in the Schools on Tuesday evenings in 1920, but by the 1930s the girls had moved to the Institute where they met from 6.30 to 9.30 on Tuesdays. The following item from a 1936 Parish Magazine not only describes a G.F.S. activity but also gives an indication of the seating capacity of the hall:

G.F.S. Missionary Evening.

The Members of the G.F.S. will give a Missionary Evening with a short Play and Lantern Pictures, in the Institute, on Tuesday, 16th March, commencing 7-30 p.m. Are there sufficient adults in the parish keen enough about the Missionary work of the Church, to fill the Institute (which holds about 100) for this occasion, thus encouraging the children in their endeavours. Hartshill as a parish is well to the fore in many things, but it lags far behind in Missionary enterprise. This is to our shame. Book the date and keep it free from other engagements. Adults, 6d.; Children, 3d.

Girl Guides

In 1953 two events took place in connection with Hartshill Girl Guides' 30th Birthday Celebrations: on Sunday, 29th November there was a dedication of the New World Flag as part of the evening service at the Parish Church and on Wednesday, 2nd December the Guides held an open night in the Institute to give people the opportunity to see how a Guide Company was run.

This means of course that there was a Guide Company in Hartshill – and presumably meeting in the Institute – from late 1923. It certainly met there in 1932, as is proved by the following extract from a letter I received from Mrs Audrey Brayford, who now lives on the Westlands:

I was born in Garner Street, Cliffe Vale in December 1931, the fourth daughter, my sisters were 11, 13 and fifteen when I arrived and all were members of the Hartshill Girl Guides who met at the institute each Wednesday evening. The Reverend R. H Wyatt had been vicar at Hartshill just a few

This picture of the 8th Stoke-on-Trent Guide Company was taken in the Institute in about 1959 when Hilary Pardoe received her Queen's Guide Award. Hilary is sitting in the centre between her mother and Assistant Divisional Commissioner Mrs Newman. The other guides sitting on the same row are, from left to right, Vivienne Evans, Anita Tempest, Kathleen Gater, Patricia Riley and Dilys Edwards. The Guide Captain, Miss Mather, is standing at the back and other guides in the picture are Margaret Butters, Pamela Dawes, Helen Jones, Pat Hemmings, Dillis Lloyd, June Munden, Susan Peake, Janet Smith and Gillian Thompson.

Photograph by courtesy of Staffordshire Sentinel News & Media
supplied by Dilys Maddocks (née Edwards)
photograph restored by Graham Yelland

weeks, my christening in January 1932 was the first he conducted there, as it was the evening of the Guides Christmas party and my eldest sister was one of my godmothers, in Guides uniform, it was suggested the Baptism party joined the Guides! I am told it was a lovely evening, especially for my dad and other males when the Vicar thought they may like to join him for a pint at one of the local hostelries!

The first mention of the Guides I have found in the Parish Magazine is from 1933 when it was reported that Mrs Brereton who had done much useful work in connection with the Guide Movement in Hartshill had tendered her resignation. This had been accepted by the Guides Commissioner, who had appointed Miss Bell to take charge of the Rangers, and Misses Cornwell and Smith to be responsible for the Guides. The article went on to say that the Rangers and Guides would be re-assembling for winter's work on Tuesday and Wednesday, September 6th and 7th, in the Institute.

Everything seemed to go well with the Guides until 1957 when Mrs Newman reported to the Church AGM that the present Captain was leaving the district and the Guides would soon be without a leader. The company had been running for well over 30 years without a break, but they had reached the stage where it would have to be closed if a Guider was not forthcoming. And, she added, without a Guide Company the Brownie Pack would be of very little use.

This unsatisfactory situation lasted for several months, but at the next AGM Mrs Newman said that the Company had obtained the services of a Lieutenant and the Guides were happy under her leadership. By 1960 things were going very well indeed. Mrs Newman was appointed Assistant Divisional Commissioner and it was reported that the Guides and Brownies were doing extremely well – as well as they had ever done at Hartshill. There was a waiting list of entrants for the Company and Pack – a rare thing in the city.

Kitchener Club

It was announced in 1935 that a Kitchener Club was to be started in the Institute for the young people of the parish, during the winter months. A new floor had been laid for the benefit of the dancing community who, it was hoped, would appreciate it and use it on every possible occasion. The club met every Saturday from 7 until 10-30 p.m. and, when it started – on Saturday, 7th September – it promised to be a great success, although there was still room for a few more members. A few weeks later something called a Long Evening was held when, the Parish Magazine reported, "apart from dancing, the members indulged in various games and competitions. Prizes were given to the most successful competitors, and a very enjoyable time was spent." However, by early 1936 the Institute Committee had decided to close the club "for the time being, owing to the lack of support from its members" and nothing more appears to have been heard of it.

Mothers' Union

The Mothers' Union met in the Institute on the first Monday of the month. In addition to providing an audience for speakers on a wide variety of subjects the members used the Institute for social evenings, Bring & Buy Sales and

This picture, which appeared in the booklet published by Hartshill Parish Church to mark its 150th Anniversary in 1992, shows the "Pageant of the Noble Woman" presented by the Mothers' Union in the Institute in 1948.

other fund raising events. In 1949 it was reported that the Mothers' Union Annual Party "was again a very jolly occasion, each member contributing to the evening's enjoyment. Judging by reports heard, the mothers did themselves remarkably well, especially regarding the refreshments, which seemed to be of good variety and plentiful supply. Possibly, sometime, an invitation might be extended to the husbands – who knows?" Whether the husbands did get the suggested invitation is not clear. Possibly not, because the next year the Vicar reported:

> The Mothers' Party was once again very enjoyable, although several members, for various reasons, were unable to be present. The tit-bit of the evening, I understand, was the splendid tea provided by the members themselves. What a feast of dainty dishes . . . trust the Mothers for that. Good luck to them for they deserve it.

So presumably the Vicar – and all the other husbands – was not invited after all. Or at least not until 1953 when "there was the usual 'feast of good things' for the inner man . . . During the evening the mothers presented the Vicar and

Mrs. Wyatt with a coffee table and a very nice electric table lamp to commemorate their twenty-one years amongst them."

Parochial Church Council

The use of the Institute, its upkeep and its finances featured quite prominently in the minutes of the Parochial Church Council from the earliest copies still extant. For example, the minutes of the meeting held on 1st July 1931 record that the Scouts were to be allowed to use the Institute on Monday evenings and that a charge of 10/6 would be made for a Whist Drive on behalf of the Cripples Guild. The charge included the 2/6 due to the caretaker.

Prior to 1935 the council met in the school but, at the June meeting that year, it was "proposed by Mr. Hyde and seconded by Mr. Beckett that commencing September 1935 the Church Council meetings be held in the Institute on the second Wednesday of the month". In fact, this decision was put into effect a couple of months earlier than that when a special meeting was held on Wednesday, 31st July attended by 21 members. The main business on the agenda was the laying of a new floor in the Institute, but the council also discussed washing down the walls after the work on the floor had been completed, the loan of trestle tables and chairs to Mr Cotton for his garden party, the formation of a Kitchener Club and the purchase of three gas rings at a cost of 9/- each.

The members of the PCC listed on the cover of the parish magazine for January 1937 are:

> *Chairman* – Rev. R. H. Wyatt; *Vice-Chairman* – Mr. F. C. Gill; *Hon. Sec.* – Mr. L. V. Boulton; Messrs. T. Smith, W. C. Barraclough, E. Aldridge, E. G. Beckett, E. Evans, A. Farrell, B. T. Hales, F.T. Hales, F. Hyde, C. H. Morley, W. Morrey, G. H. Price, S. Pratt, W. R. Stone, T. Thompson, J. Warburton; Mesdames Barraclough, Binns, Cunliffe, Dawson, B. Dawson, French, Hyde, Kerr, Liner, Mayer, Ratcliffe, Sale, Timms, Wyatt, Warburton. *St. Matthew's Representatives*: Messrs. T. Cliffe, W. Hobson, E. T. Lever Mesdames; Cliffe, Carter, Hobson, Sneyd. *Garner Street Representatives*: Messrs. Lewis, Mandley, Walton.

I quote these names merely so that I can point out that the G. H. Price listed is not me. I was only four and a half years old in January 1937.

At some time in the early fifties the frequency of meetings was cut back to once a quarter, but this did not last long. In July 1951 Mr. Morley expressed the opinion that with quarterly meetings the period between meetings was too long and there was the danger of members losing interest. As a result monthly

VOL. 47. No. 1.   **January, 1937.**   **Circulation 900.**   PRICE **2d.**

Hartshill Parish Magazine.

HOLY TRINITY CHURCH.

Clergy—The Rev. R. H. WYATT, The Vicarage ; Surrogate for granting Marriage Licences.
Curate : Rev. S. D. A. KILMISTER, B.A., 96, Princes Road.

Churchwardens—Mr. T. SMITH, " Ormonde," Newcastle Road, Penkhull ; Mr. W. BARRACLOUGH, 55, Greatbatch
Avenue, Penkhull.   **Deputy Warden**—Mr. F. T. HALES, 53a, Seabridge Road, Newcastle.

Licensed Readers—Mr. A. G. WALTON, 70, Derwent Street, Cobridge. Mr. ALFRED FARRELL, Nelson Road, Hartshill.
Mr. E. T. LEVER, Longfield Road, Hartshill.

Organist—Mr. E. S. ALDRIDGE, " Kinver," 120, Greatbatch Avenue, Penkhull.

Assistant Organist—Mrs. TIMMS, Pilgrim Cottage, Hartshill.

Choirmaster—Mr. B. T. HALES, 26, Longfield Road, Hartshill.

Hon. Magazine Organiser—Mr. F. C. GILL, 3, Egerton Road, Hartshill.

Sexton and Verger—Mr. T. SMITH, 46, Allen St., Hartshill.   **Institute Sec.**—Mr. FRED HYDE, 152, Oxford St., Penkhull.

Parochial Church Council :   Chairman—Rev. R. H. Wyatt ;   Vice-Chairman—Mr. F. C. Gill ;   Hon. Sec.—Mr. L. V.
Boulton ;   Messrs. T. Smith, W. C. Barraclough, E. Aldridge, E. G. Beckett, E. Evans, A. Farrell, B. T. Hales,
F. T. Hales, F. Hyde, C. H. Morley, W. Morrey, G. H. Price, S. Pratt, W. R. Stone, T. Thompson, J. Warburton ;
Mesdames Barraclough, Binns, Cunliffe, Dawson, B. Dawson, French, Hyde, Kerr, Liner, Mayer, Ratcliffe, Sale, Timms,
Wyatt, Warburton.   St. Matthew's Representatives : Messrs. T. Cliffe, W. Hobson, E. T. Lever ;   Mesdames Cliffe,
Carter, Hobson, Sneyd.   Garner Street Representatives :   Messrs. Lewis, Mandley, Walton.

Sidesmen :   Messrs. E. G. Beckett, T. Cliffe, E. Evans, E. Forrester, A. Farrall, F. C. Gill, B. T. Hales, B. Hawkins,
F. Hyde, A. Keech, F. Lewis, R. Peake, J. Peake, Jun., S. Pratt, G. H. Price, W. Shaw, C. E. Sillitoe, W. R.
Stone, G. Thompson, T. Thompson, W. Timms, J. Warburton, E. Wright.

ST. MATTHEW'S, KINGSCROFT.   Wardens—Messrs. T. Cliffe, W. Hobson.   **Organist**—Mr. V. Sneyd.

GARNER STREET MISSION.   Wardens—Messrs. F. Lewis, R. Mandley,   **Organist**—Mr. R. Amos.

C. H. Vyse Ltd., The Royal Printing Works, Stoke.

The cover of the Hartshill Parish Magazine for January 1937 lists G. H. Price as a member of the Parochial Church Council. It was not me. I was only four and a half years old then.

meetings were resumed from September of that year.

Notice of meetings was given in the Parish Magazine, usually accompanied by an exhortation along the lines of "Will all members please make every endeavour to be present as important business will come before the meeting". On one occasion though there was an unfortunate typographical error. In 1957 the Vicar apparently wrote "a dull attendance is asked for on Monday, 16th September", a slip which he felt he had to explain in the next issue of the magazine:

> Apology to members for the printer's error regarding the notice in last month's magazine. It should have read "a full attendance" and not a "dull attendance" as stated. Our parochial meetings are anything but "dull occasions", on the contrary they are often very lively and always enjoyable and most interesting.

And presumably they continued to be enjoyable and most interesting as long as Mr Wyatt was the Vicar. As late as November 1959 he was still expressing the hope that all the members would be present at the next meeting.

Queens

The Institute appears to have had a "royal" connection at two stages in its history: with the Queen of Hartshill in the thirties and with the Hartshill Sunday School Queen in the post-war years.

In the thirties – at least before 1939 – the "Hartshill Queen" or "Queen of Hartshill" as she was variously referred to was a young lady aged between 16 and 25 living in the Parish of Hartshill.

In 1932 the Parish Magazine reported that "The Queen of Hartshill, wearing her robes of office, with her retinue, honoured us by her presence" at the Harvest Tea, Concert and Dance, although it did not report what the lady's name was.

In 1934 the Queen's surname was reported but not her Christian name. In fact, as reported on page 31, Miss Jackson and her family organised a special event – The Queen's Effort – in the Institute that year.

The 1935 Queen was Miss Joan Hunt. On Thursday, 14th February, the men of the church choir held a whist drive in aid of the Bazaar and, the magazine reported, "the proceedings were graced by the presence of the Hartshill Queen (Miss Joan Hunt) in her robes of office, and in a felicitous manner she presented the prizes at the conclusion of the evening, consisting of numerous pieces of Wedgwood Ware."

The 1936 Queen was chosen at the Leap Year Carnival Dance held in the Institute on Thursday, 16th April, and crowned at a garden party at the

Vicarage on Thursday, 2nd July. The Queen that year was Miss Dorothy Tideswell.

By 1939, when a "Black-out" Social was held in the Institute "with curtains drawn and the windows and lights shaded, thus preventing any light to be seen from the outside", the young lady's title had changed to the "Sunday School Queen" and she was presumably younger than the earlier queens. Certainly ten years later, when Hilary Myatt (see photograph opposite) was chosen at a meeting held in the Institute to be the Hartshill Parish Church Sunday School Queen for the ensuing year she was only twelve years old.

Scouts

The Scouts' connection with the Institute went back at least to 1920 (see page 24) but it did not continue long into the thirties and the group's relationship with certain sections of the Church was not entirely a happy one. While the Scouts' contribution to Institute funds through their concerts was reported in glowing terms in 1932, a couple of years later the Parochial Church Council received a complaint from the Institute caretaker about damage to chairs, interference with the clock and chairs in the gallery, loosening of the recently repaired handrail to the staircase, finger marks on the walls and he added that when he arrived at 10 p.m. to close the Institute he could not get the Scouts to leave before 10.25 or 10.30 p.m.

At a subsequent meeting the Institute Secretary said the Committee had inspected the damage previously reported to the Council and that the work required to be done consisted of cleaning the marks from the walls and repairing the staircase handrail. As the damage was less serious than anticipated it was decided that the Scouts should not be asked to pay for this work. As far as the complaint about closing time was concerned, the Scoutmaster, Mr. B. Hales, said this was never later than 10.10 p.m. and that the Institute was only used fortnightly after 9.30 p.m.

The whole situation was resolved later that year when the Vicar reported that new headquarters had been arranged for the Scouts at Harpfield School and that after 1st January 1935 they would not require the use of the Institute any more.

St John Ambulance

The Hartshill unit of the St John Ambulance Brigade met at the Institute on Friday evenings. In 1940 the brigade was charged a rental of £5 a year. In 1948 an appeal was made in the parish magazine for young men of 16 and over to come along to the Institute on Friday, 19th November to learn how they could

The 1949 Sunday School Queen, Hilary Myatt, with her attendants Pat Turner, Pamela Walford, Carol Yoxall, Joan Pashley and Barbara Pashley.

Photograph by B. & B. Photo Specialists of Hartshill supplied by Hilary Baxter (née Myatt)

become first-aiders. A couple of years later a Cadet Division was formed. This time the call was for boys between the ages of 11 and 15. This was coupled with an "appeal to all parents to encourage their boys to join the Cadet movement, where the boys would mix together and be taught how to be useful in cases of accident or illness, either at home, school or in the street."

In neither of these cases was their any reference to girls or young women. Yet girls were obviously admitted too, as is proved by the memories of June Watt (née Wain) who told me that it was at St John meetings in the Institute that she learnt how to use triangular and roller bandages, how to apply splints to broken limbs and even how to improvise a splint using the branch of a tree, all of which was valuable grounding for her later career as a nurse.

In view of the questions raised by these brief references to St John in church documents I sought advice from St John's Staffordshire headquarters whose archivist, Terry Millington, was able to add some further details. These, in turn, raised other questions – for example about what went on at the Institute in the forties – which neither Terry nor I have been able to resolve.

According to records held by St John there was a cadet division which met at the Hartshill Institute from 1951 to 1961, when it moved to Harpfields School. It was originally known as Stoke No. 2 Cadet Division but, when men joined in 1953, the name was shortened to Stoke No. 2 Division. Terry has not been able to trace when ladies were admitted but he did comment that men did first aid and ladies did nursing, the men being referred to as Ambulance Members and the ladies as Ambulance Sisters.

Sunday School

Although I found no reference to it in either the Parochial Church Council minutes or the Parish Magazine, I have been told by one of my contacts that Sunday School classes took place in the Institute in the 1940s and 1950s. He couldn't remember how many years he attended the classes, but he had a clear memory of the children sitting around the fireplace (see opposite page) in a semi-circle to keep warm in winter.

Whist Drives

As mentioned in Chapter 5, whist drives were already frequent social events before the Wyatt years. In 1932 weekly whist drives were started and the Vicar commented: "These are very homely and enjoyable. If you have not hitherto attended same, do so as soon as possible, they are well worth your presence and support." There were even occasional whist drives during the summer as the following note from 1934 shows:

WHIST DRIVE.

On Thursday, July 5th, 7-30 p m., on Vicarage Lawn (if fine) but if wet – in the Institute. Proceeds towards Choir Boys' Holiday Camp. Admission 1/- (including Refreshments).

Over the years enthusiasm ebbed and flowed. In 1935 the Vicar felt the need to appeal for more support, adding: "Unless this support is forthcoming they will have to be discontinued." But the following year the PCC approved the purchase of two dozen new whist tables and whist drives were still being held as late as the early fifties – with fluctuating levels attendance – raising money for various causes, including the Institute itself as this note from 1950 shows:

Whist Drives.

During July, Whist Drives will be held in the Institute on Mondays, 3rd, 10th and 24th July, at 7-30 p.m., when we hope all our players will be out in

The Institute fireplace as it now is. It has obviously not been used for a very long time – possibly getting on for half a century.

full force. The Proceeds from the 'drives' is to defray the expenses of the new heating apparatus recently installed in the institute, so please do your best to come along and support a worthy cause.

A couple of months later this was followed with the encouraging news that:

With the new boiler installed in the Institute it should now be possible to have a warmer room in which to play whist during the winter months. We have quite a nice party who come regularly to the drives and quite an enjoyable evening is spent together. There will be whist drives held on Mondays, 13th and 27th November, to which we heartily invite any player who would like to join our happy throng. The drives commence at 7-30 p.m. and run straight through without an interval so that players are out in good time to catch their various 'buses.

Youth Club

The minutes of the Parochial Church Council record that in March 1954 "Mr. Parkes asked if the Institute could be used for a Youth Cub on Thursday evenings after the First Aid People have vacated it at 8.30 p.m. He said that Mr. Gwilt of the St. John's Ambulance Brigade could be out by 8.45 p.m. and the room would be required until 10.30 p.m."* The PCC agreed to this request and initially allowed the Youth Club to use the Institute free of charge for six months between 8.45 p.m. and 10.30 p.m. on Thursday evenings providing it was not required by the St. John Ambulance Brigade or one of the Church Organisations. At the end of the first six months period Mr. Parkes reported that the club was doing well and their small committee had decided that weekly contributions should be paid for the purchase of a billiard table, skittle table and table tennis equipment. About 30 members attended regularly and paid 6d per night. The PCC agreed to the club continuing to use the Institute free of charge for a further six months after which a rental at the same rate at least as the other organisations would be charged. However, in January 1955 the club voluntarily paid two guineas to cover its use of the Institute up to 31st December 1954 and this was followed by a further £10 in April.

Non-Parochial Activities

People who grew up in Hartshill in the period between the early 1930s and the mid-1960s remember the Institute being used by other sections of the Church, other than those specifically mentioned, for meetings, parties, concerts and so on. In addition the Institute was also used for a number of purposes which were not strictly connected with the Church. One of the people who contacted me with memories commented that the Institute was "a busy little place during the war; it was the hub of the village in those days". In fact, she added, in addition to all the other things that went on there it was the assembly point for the Air Raid Wardens before they went about their nightly ARP duties.

Long before this, though, the Parochial Church Council had discussed what it described as "Non-Parochial" use of the Institute and, at its meeting on 17th September 1931 it decided that the charges for such use would be:

12 noon to 11 p.m.	£1.1.0	+ 5/- piano + 2/6 caretaker
5 p.m. to 11 p.m.	15/-	+ 5/- piano + 2/6 caretaker
2/6 per hour after 11 p.m.		+ 6d per hour for caretaker

For Meetings	2/6 per hour – minimum 10/-
Afternoon letting	2/6 per hour – minimum 10/-

It was also suggested that a notice be inserted in the parish magazine pointing

---

* I found the mention of the St John Ambulance Brigade rather puzzling, as all other references were to St John meeting on Friday not Thursday (see page 44).

out that the room was available for such meetings, but unfortunately there are no copies of the magazine of that time extant, so we have no means of knowing how the availability of the room was publicised.

The basic charges for parochial use were about half the above, but the piano and caretaker supplements were the same.

Conservatives

In June 1939 The Vicar informed the PCC that he had received a request from the "Juvenile Conservative Branch" for the hire the Institute on the first Tuesday afternoon in each month from 2.30 p.m. to 5 p.m. This was approved subject to payment being made in accordance with the scale of charges in operation. There is no further reference in the PCC minutes to the use of the Institute by this – or any other political party – until 1954 when the Vicar reported that an enquiry had been received from the Penkhull Conservative Association about the price that would be charged for the hire of the Institute for a whist drive on Tuesdays between the hours of 2.30 p.m. and 4.30 p.m. The response of the PCC was that the charge would be £1.1.0. plus a charge for broken crockery on the first occasion and on future occasions a charge would be made for the use of crockery.

Dancing Classes

On Saturday mornings in the fifties Irene Kelsall, who lived in Basford Park Road, ran a dancing class for children. The photograph on page 50 was taken in 1951 during one of these classes but my informant, Tricia Johnson (née Mancell), was not old enough at the time to remember much about it. She is the baby near the right of the picture sitting on her sister Christine's knee.

Education Department

The City Education Department possibly used the Institute for two purposes in the forties and fifties: school meals and physical training. I say 'possibly' because I have not been able to determine whether the first use actually took place.

School Meals

In 1942 the Education authorities applied to use of the Institute and St. Andrews Mission as "feeding centres for school children". This meant, the Vicar reported to the PCC, that the Institute would have to be cleaned and

Children attending a Saturday morning dancing class in the Institute in the early fifties.
Photograph supplied by Tricia Johnson (née Mancell)

redecorated, but I have not been able to trace any further reference to this happening at that time.

Some years later – in 1950 – the Education Committee approached the Council again about using the Institute "on approximately five days per week throughout the year between the hours of 11.30 a.m. and 2.30 p.m. (with the possible exception of Wakes Week and Christmas Week) for the purpose of serving school meals." A sub-committee was set up to look into this and, after a couple of meetings, reported that in view of the alterations to the building, which the Education Dept. would require, plus the fact that a full-time caretaker would have to be appointed (quite apart from the increased cost of heating, lighting, etc) the lowest figure which could be accepted as rent for the use of the room was £200 per year. The Education Committee's response to this was that, "as the number of children using the Hall would not warrant the hiring at the rent proposed, the question of the establishment of a Feeding Centre in the district would have to be deferred." And, it seems, nothing more was heard of this proposal.

Physical Training

Physical Training was a different matter. This first arose in 1940, early in World War II, when the erection of air-raid shelters at Hartshill C of E Primary

School had deprived it of space for physical training – or drill, as it was called at the time. The headmaster asked if the Institute could be used for this purpose on Friday afternoons and it was left to him to agree with the Education Department how much rent would be paid. The figure agreed would appear to have been £7.10.0 per year.

In April 1953 the Vicar informed the Council that for some years past the school had been using the Institute on Thursday mornings, Friday mornings and Friday afternoons for physical training at the 1940 annual rent of £7.10.0 and he felt it was time to ask the Education Authority for an increase in view of the considerable increase in costs that had occurred in the meantime. This was taken up with the Education Authority which said that it was prepared to pay £10 a year. The Parochial Church Council was not impressed by this offer and replied saying that it considered "the offer to be inadequate in view of the greatly increased cost of heating, lighting, etc. since the agreement was entered into". It asked for £20 per year which the Education Committee agreed to pay from 1st June 1953. This did not last long though, for less than a year later the Town Clerk gave formal notice of the Education Committee's intention to terminate its use of the Institute on 31st March 1954.

Independent Order of Foresters

In 1933 the Penkhull Court of the Independent Order of Foresters applied for permission to use the Institute on the first Wednesday and third Monday of each month and offered to pay £9 per annum. This was accepted by the PCC for a period of twelve months, subject to three months notice on either side, payments to be made quarterly and a proper agreement being made. I have not been able to find out how long this arrangement lasted, although there was a complaint from the Foresters after a few weeks about draught from the skylight.

Wedding Receptions

I mentioned the wedding reception of John and Lulu Barstow in the previous chapter. That was in 1927, but the Institute continued to be used for wedding receptions for many years after that. Two ladies in particular contacted me to tell me about their own receptions.

Joan Bennett married Edmund Webb at Holy Trinity Church on Saturday, 19th September 1942 and the reception was held in the Institute. "We did the catering ourselves," she commented, "because that was what you did in those days."

When Joyce Millington married Alan Lambert on Thursday, 31st March 1960 the Vicar would not allow the ceremony to take place at Holy Trinity

Joyce Millington and Alan Lambert (right) met at one of the Saturday night dances, which were being run in the fifties by Joyce's uncle, Jim Parkes. As they both lived just outside Hartshill parish, the wedding ceremony on Thursday, 31st March 1960 could not take place at Holy Trinity Church, but the reception was held in the Institute. After Alan's death, Joyce remarried.

Photo supplied by Joyce Charlton (formerly Lambert, née Millington)

because, in spite of their strong connections with the church, they both lived just outside Hartshill parish. The actual wedding was at St. Peter's in Stoke, but the reception was held in the Institute (see picture above) because it was a place that held very important memories for Mr and Mrs Lambert. Joyce's uncle, Jim Parkes, assisted by his wife Doris, ran the Saturday night dances at the Institute at the time and it was there that Joyce and Alan met.

7. The 1960s

The Reverend R H Wyatt decided to retire in April 1960. His wife Nellie, whom he described as labouring "for many years as an unpaid curate", had died a few weeks earlier and he felt that without her he could not carry on in his post. Writing in that month's issue of the Parish Magazine he said:

> Over a period of twenty-nine years I have been privileged to write the monthly letter for the parish magazine as Vicar of Hartshill but this will be the last one, for as you already know I am retiring as from April 18th. I have always thought the magazine to be a happy medium between the parish Priest and the People committed to his care. It gives one the opportunity of bringing to the notice of all parishioners details regarding our religion, various festivals of the church, our worship and services, as well as the many activities connected with the spiritual and social life of the community. It also records special events and functions held throughout . . . the parish in general.

Mr Wyatt's reports have been of great value to me in researching what went on at the Institute during those years. As mentioned in the previous chapter documentary evidence for the next few years – up to its acquisition by the Newcastle Players in 1969 – is rather thin on the ground. Also very few people have contacted me with personal memories of that period.

The latest relevant issues of the magazine held in the Minton Centre are for 1964 and they indicate that several organisations were still using the Institute at that time such as the Mothers' Union (First Monday in each month at 7-30 p.m.), Youth Club (Every Tuesday at 7-30 p.m.), Brownies (Every Wednesday at 6 p.m.), Girl Guides (Every Wednesday at 7-30 p.m.) and C.E.M.S. (First Thursday in each month at 7-45 p.m.). Possibly the Women's Fellowship (Third Thursday at 7-30 p.m.) also met in the Institute. What I do know is that the Women's Fellowship held a Jumble Sale in the Institute at 6 p.m. on Friday, 20th March 1964.

There are no Parochial Church Council minutes extant referring to the Institute later than the autumn of 1960. They do, however, report that the Parish Church Harvest Supper was to be held on Monday, 3rd October 1960 starting at 7.15 pm with tickets at 2/6 each. At the September PCC meeting the Vicar – the Reverend Frank W. Hickling, who had recently succeeded Mr

The Reverend Frank W. Hickling.
Photograph by courtesy of Holy Trinity Church, Hartshill

Wyatt and held the post until 1971 – "expressed the view that this should be a parish effort and he hoped the Institute would be full on this occasion".

I have, however, been able to glean some more information from the Annual General Meeting minutes for the period:

C.E.M.S.

In 1961 Mr Tulley reported that membership was static. They were not going forward unfortunately. They were doing their best to attract new members and to get men interested in the monthly meetings which were largely devoted to discussions. If the stewardship scheme was a success spiritually it could be anticipated that more members could be attracted to the branch which, as the body, could give considerable support the work of the parish. Financially the year's working had resulted in a loss but there was still a small working balance in hand.

The following year the report was given to the AGM by Mr J. Hancock. The number of members had increased; they had had a fairly active year and most members had played a very active role in the Christian Stewardship Campaign; the meetings had been fairly well attended and they had received great help from the Vicar and Mrs. Hickling, but they would like to see more members. In fact, in 1964 and 1965 Mr Hancock said that average attendance at meetings was only nine.

Girl Guides and Brownies

The Girl Guides and Brownies were thriving in 1961. There was a regular membership of 30 Guides and 36 Brownies with a list of young people waiting to join. The only other reference to the Guides and Brownies was in 1963 when Miss Mather reported that since Christmas she had no longer been connected with the Guides and they now had a new Captain. They were doing exceptionally well, she said, and at Christmas they had once more made up parcels for the old people.

Carole Bissell (née Hopwood) of the Porthill Players recalls joining the Brownies while they were still meeting in the Institute. The Brown Owl at that time was Mrs Stocks who lived in the detached house (now 263 Hartshill Road) at the far end of the Minton Cottages. She had a daughter Katie who was a contemporary of Carole's in the Brownies.

Mothers' Union

Reports on the Mothers' Union during this period were made by Mrs Hickling, the Vicar's wife. They were generally along the lines that the organisation was in a very healthy state. The usual meetings had been held during the year including a joint meeting with the C.E.M.S. In 1963 the Mothers' Union was getting along very happily. They had one or two young members and meetings were well attended on the whole, but there was plenty of room for new members. A year later they were still hoping for new members.

Youth Club

In 1961 the Youth Club was very healthy. John Pedrazzini, who now lives in Hanford, was a committee member then and he still has the register from that time. It contains the names of about 100 young people between the ages of 12 and 17 from Hartshill, Harpfields, Penkhull, Cliffe Vale and Basford, about eighty of whom attended each week.

The club met on Tuesday evenings and admission was sixpence which had to be paid at the hatch in the inside wooden wall to the right of the front door. In fact the whole of the area behind that wall under the balcony including the spiral staircase was screened off using scenery belonging to the Hartshill Entertainers. This cubbyhole was used as a committee room. There was also a tuck shop there where one of the girls sold bottles of pop from a stall under the stairs – a rather hazardous enterprise as she frequently banged her head on the iron stairs.

Music was provided using a very old Vox valve amplifier coupled to a modern BSR record deck with a speaker in front of the balcony and two more either side the stage at the other end of the hall.

On one occasion the club ran its own version of the popular BBC television programme *Juke Box Jury*. The Vicar's wife, Mrs Hickling, was a member of the jury which was chaired by one of the girls, Pat Hemmings. They were planning to use *Hit and Miss*, the John Barry theme tune from the television show, but somebody had wired the speakers directly into the mains which blew them up. "That really annoyed me," said John Pedrazzini – and that's probably quite an understatement. "Anyway, these things happen, don't they?" he added.

Another problem was getting the members to go home at the end of the evening. It was supposed to finish at ten o'clock but they proved reluctant to leave at that time – until somebody came up with the idea of playing the National Anthem. "By the time it was finished," John recalled, "most of them had gone."

At the 1962 Annual General Meeting Miss Mather said that the Youth Club had experienced a very up-and-down year. The attempt to paint the Institute had not been a great success but they were hoping to finish the work some time soon. Attendance had dropped to about thirty a week.

I could find no more references to the Youth Club in any of the documents I have been able to consult.

The last AGM at the Institute

The first Annual General Meeting the Rev Frank W. Hickling chaired was in 1961 and the last AGM meeting held in the Institute was on Monday, 15th March 1965.

In his opening remarks at the 1965 AGM the Vicar, Mr Hickling, "recalled many events which had happened during the previous year, i.e. the closing of the Church School and taking over by the Church". There were the usual reports from the Brownies (mentioning that further help was required in connection with the Guides), Women's Fellowship, Mothers' Union and C.E.M.S. but no indication of where the meetings were being held at that time.

However, the Vicar did mention that "in the event of the School Hall not being available at the time of the Deanery Festival it was thought we could probably hire the Medical Institute at Hartshill", which suggests that the Institute was no longer in use by the Church then.

And so, it would seem, the Institute stood empty and unused from some time in the mid-1960s until 1969 when it was sold to the Newcastle Players. At the Church's Annual General Meeting the following year the Vicar mentioned that the proceeds from the sale of the Institute would be used to install a new central heating plant at the Church Hall.

8. Fabric and Finance before 1969

At the start of this book I mentioned a photograph showing Holy Trinity Church, Hartshill at some time in the 1940s that appeared our local newspaper, *The Sentinel*, in June 2007 in its *JIM MORGAN'S MYSTERY PICTURE* series. It was taken looking from the vicinity of what was then called The Hartshill Church Institute. I have traced several pictures of this nature. For example the eminent local historian and photographer, E. J. D. Warrillow, included a similar view, taken on a snowy winter's day, in his book *A Sociological History of Stoke-on-Trent* (1960) and there are other pictures of the same type in the Warrillow Collection held at Keele University. However, I have not been able to trace a photograph of the exterior of the building earlier than the one on the opposite page which was published in the booklet celebrating the 150th Anniversary of Hartshill Church in 1992. It does not tell us much about the building, but in any case the vehicles in the picture would suggest that it was taken no earlier than the 1950s.

When the building was opened in 1859, both *The Staffordshire Sentinel* and *The Staffordshire Advertiser* contained detailed descriptions of it, inside and out. The following is a shortened version based on these two reports, but retaining much of the nineteenth century wording:

> The building is Gothic in style, partaking in its general outline as well as in its details, of the Italian treatment of Gothic, as being better adapted to the proportions required. It comprises a reading-room or lecture-hall about 46 feet by 23 feet and a commodious residence for the hall keeper adjoining.
>
> The front of the hall forms a gable to the Newcastle Road, the adjoining keeper's house occupying the same frontage, but slightly receding from the extreme line of front. The gable is roofed over with a timber framing, similar in style, though different in design, to that of the new cottages close by. The main front of the reading room is in brick, but highly relieved by white and grey stone, black brick, marble, wood, and a black and red tiles, the whole of these varied materials being blended together in excellent harmony, and with artistic effect. The tympanum of each window is filled with a beautiful diaper in black and red indented tiles by Minton and Co., and look as if carved in that material. A rose window is introduced in the gable, the timber framing of which is also novel, and harmonises well with the peculiarly picturesque ensemble of the range of cottages lately completed from the design of Mr. George Gilbert Scott.

This picture, which appeared in the booklet published by Hartshill Parish Church to mark its 150th Anniversary in 1992, shows the Institute with the Campbell cottages to the right. The Standard 8 in the foreground indicates that it was probably taken in the 1950s,

Between the hall and the keeper's house, a turret rises to the height of 40 feet, covered in with Minton's roofing tiles, in red and chocolate colours. This turret forms the porch of the dwelling, and also contains the stair to the gallery, which is situated at the front end of the hall.

The entrance to the hall is through a spacious arched doorway, the arch being supported by Purbeck marble columns, ornamented by Caen stone, the Gable bearing the monogram of Mr Campbell, in appropriate characters.

The roof is an open timbered one, and perhaps the most original and effective part of the design. A lantern, constructed in it, supplies the room with abundant and agreeable light, while a row of quatrefoils running round the top of the lantern, carries off the vitiated air.

A permanent platform is erected at the end, opposite the entrance, and the front of it is hung with doors enclosing a range of shelving for the books of the classes &c. Doors are placed at each end, for egress from the hall on the right, and on the left for communication with the keeper's house.

Access from the 'stair to the gallery' was probably through a door or doorway. At some time in the building's history this was bricked up and plastered over

On the left Minton tiles set into the doorway and on the right a section of the facade including Colin Minton Campbell's monogram over the front door.

so that its exact location cannot now be seen. To get up to the gallery now there is a spiral staircase that is so tight that nineteenth century ladies in their voluminous dresses would have found it impossible to negotiate. Bricking up the doorway was perhaps not completely approved of for, when the Newcastle Players bought the building in 1969, our then President, John Barstow, regaled us with a tales of a ghostly figure which was reputed to pass through the wall to the adjoining cottage and stand on the gallery looking down on what was going on down below.

But that is the subject of a later chapter in this book.

We have no architect's drawings showing the original layout of the building , but the drawing opposite was, I believe, drawn at the time of our Lottery application (see page 98) and shows the ground floor layout.

The photograph on page 62 which I think I took in 1980 shows the building more or less as it is today. There are, however, some facts about the frontage of the Institute as it used to be that are worth commenting on.

The newspaper reports of the official opening refer to the arch over the

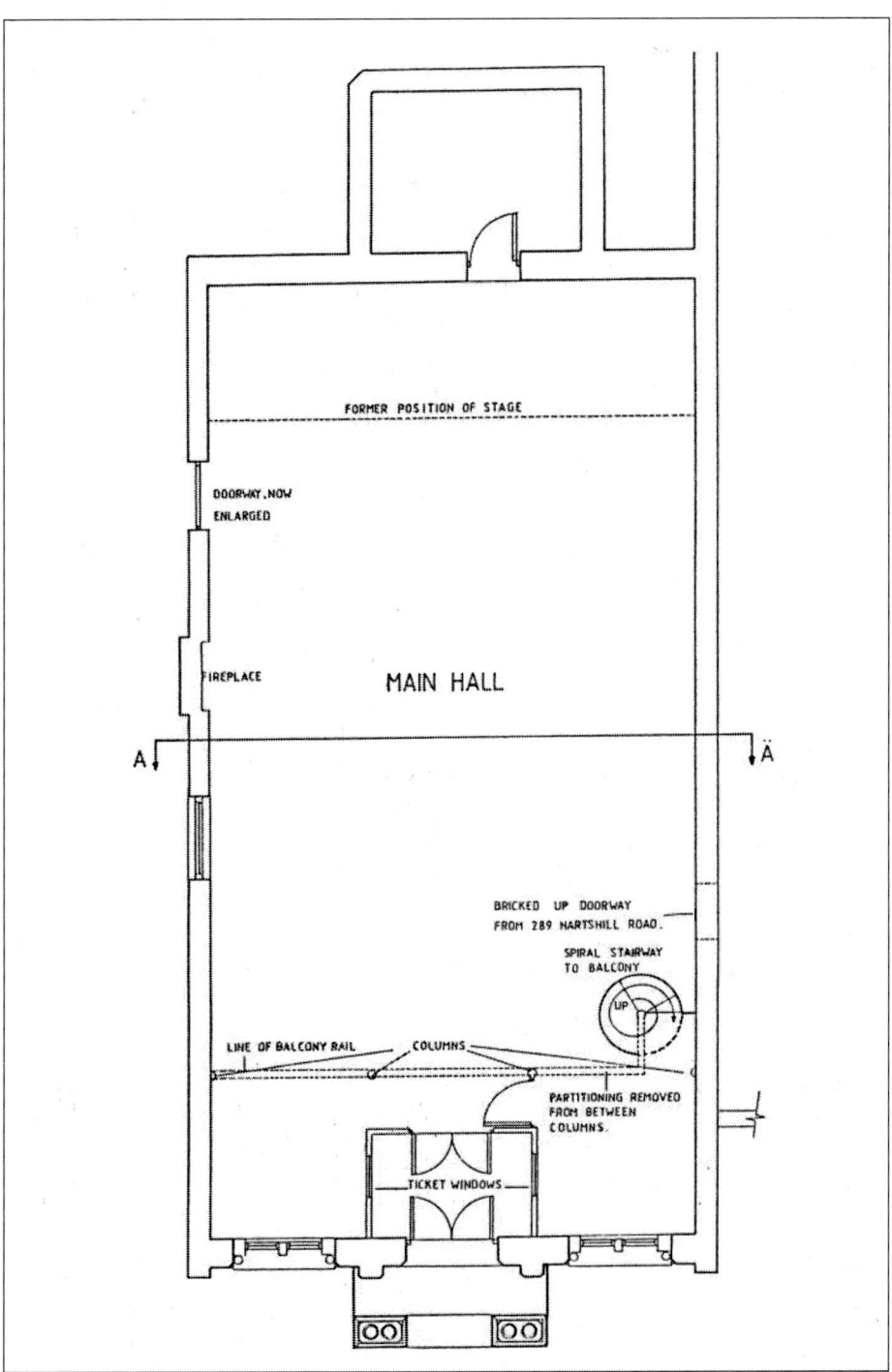

FORMER POSITION OF STAGE

DOORWAY, NOW ENLARGED

FIREPLACE

MAIN HALL

A

Ä

BRICKED UP DOORWAY FROM 289 HARTSHILL ROAD.

SPIRAL STAIRWAY TO BALCONY

UP

LINE OF BALCONY RAIL

COLUMNS

PARTITIONING REMOVED FROM BETWEEN COLUMNS.

TICKET WINDOWS

The photograph above was probably taken in 1980. It shows the frontage of the building more or less as it is today, although it is now in a much better state of preservation than it was then. Also the doors are now painted black and white rather than the horrible shade of yellow we originally chose. The fact that our then President, John Barstow, insisted that the correct name for the colour was gamboge did not make it any less horrible.

front entrance being supported by Purbeck marble columns. Yet in September 1934 it was noted by the Parochial Church Council that "the plaster to the pillars of the porch outside the front entrance doors is falling away in places", so what happened in the intervening 75 years to the marble columns? Were they really plaster-coated columns made to look like marble? Whatever the answer, nothing was done about the columns until April 1936 when Bailey & Berrisford of Fenton were asked to look into the problem. They recommended that the old plaster be removed from the pillars and that they be resurfaced with cement. It was estimated that this would cost between £8 and £10. Again no action appears to have been taken.

In 1938 the PCC was occupied with possible changes to the Institute at both the front and rear of the building.

Land at the rear came up for sale and the Vicar wondered if it was worth buying it for possible future extensions. The Finance Committee was commissioned to look into the matter but in October 1938 it recommended "that the purchase of the land at the rear of the Institute be not entertained".

At one time there was not only a low wall in front of the Institute but also iron railings and a gate or gates. In 1938 Stoke-on-Trent City Council decided to widen Hartshill Road and to do this it needed to purchase a strip of land outside the Institute from the Church. The Parochial Church Council apparently agreed to forego compensation for the loss of land provided Stoke-on-Trent Corporation would "set back the existing gate posts on to the new line and erect new gates and swing the same across the entrance." A letter from the District Valuer dated 9th July 1938 says: "I understand that you prefer twin gates to enable them to fasten in the centre rather than one swing gate attached and swung from one of the gate posts."

In spite of this, money did change hands and the sale of the "small strip of land containing 4½ square yards in front if the Mission Room (sic) to the Stoke-on-Trent Corporation" was completed in March 1939 and a cheque for £2: 0: 0d was paid to the Vicar and Churchwardens "for use in connection with the Mission Room". The corporation had also agreed "to set back the boundary wall and rail fence to the new improvement Line and to re-erect the existing gate on the said Line and make it good."

The railings, however, were short-lived in their new position. The Second World War saw to that. In April 1942 the Vicar informed the PCC that under the new defence regulations the power to requisition iron railings had been granted to the local authorities and the Institute railings had already been earmarked for collection. So that was the end of the railings. The only evidence that they ever existed is a metal fixing stub in one of the plinths below the porch pillars and evidence that there were originally two of these stubs in each plinth.

The boarded-up window at the side of the building . . . . . .

The poor state of these pillars came to the attention of the PCC again in September 1951. Meiklejohns of Stoke and Stephen Heath of Newcastle were asked to quote and their estimates were as follows:

Meiklejohn & Sons Ltd, Stoke	New octagon columns	£17.14. 0.
	New circular ditto	£24. 0. 0.
Stephen Heath & Son, Newcastle	New circular columns	£89.18. 0.

This time the work was put in hand and, not surprisingly, it was decided that "the estimate of Messrs Meiklejohn & Sons for the provision of new octagon columns, amounting to £17.14. 0. be accepted." The cement coated columns can clearly be seen in the photograph on page 62.

In July 1953, it was noted that the boundary wall at the rear of the passage behind the Institute was in a dilapidated condition. This wall retains the high ground at the rear of the Institute and as far as the Parochial Church Council could ascertain it was – and presumably still is – the responsibility of the owners who have access to the passage to carry out any repairs necessary. The Vicar promised to get in touch with Dr. Richards who owned the land at the rear in an effort to get him to contribute towards the cost. The Vicar and

. . . . . . and the same window seen from inside. There is still glass in the upper panes.

Wardens were given authority to deal with the matter as required but, frustratingly, there is no further mention of it in the PCC minutes. However, judging by the state of the wall now, more than fifty years later, it would be fair to assume that nothing was done about it.

When the Newcastle Players bought the building in 1969 the windows at the front and side were already boarded up. I have not been able to trace when this happened, but it is probable that there was still glass in them at the start of the Second World War. As early as November 1939 the minutes of the Parochial Church Council record that "The existing blackout of the Institute Windows not having proved satisfactory, it was decided to have Curtains made for the Side, Back and Cloak Room windows". The cost of blacking out the Institute was to be met from the Institute Account.

The hall may have been blacked out, but all was not gloom and doom as the following extract from the parish magazine shows:

A "Black-out" Social.
With curtains drawn and the windows and lights shaded, thus preventing any light to be seen from the outside, a very jolly and enjoyable Social, organised by the Sunday School teachers, was held in the Institute on

Thursday, November 16th. Social enjoyment, under supervised conditions, was the order of the evening. Dancing, games, comic plays, and various competitions, gave amusement to suit all classes and ages. Refreshments provided during the interval gave great satisfaction in these days of food restrictions. The hall was crowded with a merry party who when warmed up, took part in everything going on. They were out for a good time and certainly got it. The Sunday School Queen presented the prizes to the winners of the games and competitions, etc. We offer our sincere thanks to those responsible for the evening's enjoyment. It was decided to hold another similar occasion in the near future.

Early in 1940 a discussion took place about the advisability of removing the dark paint from the Institute windows now that black-out curtains had been provided and it was decided that this should be done on the understanding that the heads of all organisations using the room must be responsible for drawing the dark curtains when they were using the room.

It would appear that interior decoration of the hall had not been finished when it was officially opened on 10th January 1859, although the two local newspapers did not agree on its actual state. The *Sentinel* report stated that "the walls are, at present, bare" while the *Advertiser* wrote: "the walls internally . . . at present are merely coloured in distemper." Both, though, reported that the walls were to be "plastered and painted decoratively in *fresco*" over the ensuing months. A couple of days later, when what was described as "the second inauguration meeting" took place, the hall had, in the words of the *Sentinel*, "undergone a perfect and almost surprising metamorphosis . . . Instead of bare walls and murky looking forms, the former were literally covered with beautiful paintings and engravings."

We do not know what the "*fresco*" decoration looked like, but since 1859 the hall has been decorated quite a few times. In October 1891, for example, the *Stoke-on-Trent Parish Magazine* expressed the hope that the Institute would soon "present a habitable appearance". A tender for the painting and renovation of the interior had been accepted and the work was to be put in hand almost immediately. That this was done is borne out by the report two months later that the Social Club had given an Evening Party in the Institute, on Thursday, 19th November, "which was much enjoyed by all present". The room had been "lately painted and decorated by the Club, and looked bright and comfortable for the occasion."

Painting and decorating the Institute featured at intervals in the proceedings of the Parochial Church Council over the years.

In the summer of 1933 a breakdown of necessary painting and renovation work was presented to the Council:

Repairs	about £14	
Outside painting	about £12	
Inside painting	about £24	
If inside walls are painted 3 coats	about £4-10-0	extra
If papered	about £2-5-0	extra

The work was carried out and at the PCC's September meeting Mr Hyde reported that "the Institute Committee considered the work to be done satisfactorily." It had in fact cost £54.10.0 which suggests that the inside walls had not been papered but had received three coats of paint.

It was to be nearly twenty years before the question of the internal decoration of the Institute arose again. At the Church's 1952 Annual General Meeting the Vicar commented that the Institute needed money spending on it for re-furnishing and redecoration. This resulted in the PCC obtaining estimates from several decorating firms but an architect's survey carried out at the time revealed that certain structural repairs needed doing before the redecoration could proceed. These included replacing slates adjoining the chimney stack, repointing the flashings, and unblocking and cleaning the condensation grooves and pipes. It was also suggested that louvres be inserted in the lantern light to prevent condensation which was causing dampness in the roof beams. The cost of this work was £38.10.0.

Redecoration was not mooted again until 1956 when the following estimates were received:

F. T. Hales & Co. Ltd, Hartshill	£107. 0. 0.
Lawton Bros, Hartshill	£110. 0. 0.
P. J. Penson Ltd, Hartshill	£119.17. 6.
J. Massey & Son, Hanley	£135. 0. 0.

The lowest tender was accepted and the Institute was closed for three weeks to allow the work to be done. The Vicar was obviously very satisfied with the result but, as the following two extracts from the Parish Magazine show, he felt that some users of the building could exercise more care in their use of it:

Institute Notice
Now that the Institute has been painted and re-decorated will the Leaders of all Organisations please see that their members do not mess up the walls, sit on the fireguard or misuse the card tables. More care must be taken of the chairs and repairs to broken chairs in future will be charged to the organisation concerned.

Institute. I would like to remind Leaders of the various organisations using the Institute to keep a strict watch on their members regarding the newly-painted walls, as already they show the signs of someone's dirty hands across them. You will appreciate that the P.C.C. has just paid over one hundred pounds to have the Institute painted and decorated we don't want to have it messed up by careless members using it.

Could careless members 'messing up' the Institute have been the reason why the Youth Club attempted to paint it in 1961 or 1962. As mentioned on page 56 this had not been a great success and was not completed at the time of the 1962 AGM. I wonder if they did finish the job.

As mentioned in Chapter 6, during the summer of 1935 the PCC decided that the Institute floor had become unsuitable for dances. This matter was probably the most important item on the agenda of a special meeting of the Council held on Wednesday, 31st July that year. It was in fact the first PCC meeting to be held in the Institute. The relevant section of the minutes of this meeting is reproduced verbatim on the panel opposite.

Another item on the agenda of that special meeting was the Institute Gas Stove. This was presumably a cooking stove, for it was reported that the Secretary of the Institute Committee stated that at the previous meeting of the Council it had been decided to purchase a new hot plate. He said he had interviewed an official of the Gas Dept. who had advised the purchase of three gas rings at a cost of nine shillings each, the rings to be screwed down to a board which would fit the existing fixture. After some discussion the Council decided to rescind its previous resolution to purchase a hot plate and to buy three gas rings instead.

Heating in general was problem feature of the Institute throughout its history – right up to the present day in fact.

There is a fireplace on the outside wall of the Institute (see pictures on pages 47 and 73). Ladies who attended the Saturday night dances remember that the young men used to congregate around it to warm themselves – and no doubt discuss the female talent present – while the girls danced with each other. But a small fireplace could not generate enough heat to keep the whole room warm. Some form of general heating was, and always has been, necessary. This, we believe, was generated in a boiler house located under the kitchen and accessed from outside down steps and through a door at the back of the building (see photograph on page 70).

In February 1891 *Stoke-on-Trent Parish Magazine* reported on the purchase of a new boiler as follows:

> It is only due to the Committee of the Working Men's Club to state that they have just recently spent over £12 in putting in a new boiler, and securing the efficiency of the heating apparatus of the Institution. The benefit is mainly

Extract from the minutes of a
Special Council Meeting
8 p.m. Wed. 31 July 1935 in the Institute.

Estimates for the new floor at Institute

Mr. Gill informed the Council that a suggestion had been made to him that instead of laying a new wood floor a patent cement composition should be laid on the existing boards. After considerable discussion it was decided to lay a new boarded floor in accordance with the Council's previous resolution.

The following were the estimates received:-

	New floor	New joists
Mr. B. Chesterton, Hartshill	£35. 0. 0.	3½d per ft.
Meiklejohn & Sons, Stoke	£22.10. 0.	7d per ft.
J. Tatton, Basford	£21. 0. 0.	5d per ft.
Bailey & Berrisford, Fenton	£17.18. 0.	no price given

It was pointed out that Bailey & Berrisford hadn't given a price for new joists.

Proposed by Mrs. Dawson and seconded by Mr. Thompson, that the estimate of Mr. Tatton be accepted. This was carried. It was decided that Mr. Hales be asked to superintend the work, also that the timber from the floor should be sold to a firelighter manufacturer.

Mr. Barraclough proposed that Mr. Hales be asked for an estimate of the cost of washing down the walls after the new floor had been laid. This was seconded by Mr. Carter and carried, the Vicar, the Wardens, and Institute Committee Secretary being empowered to accept the estimate if considered reasonable.

The actual minutes were handwritten and the full minutes of the meeting of 31st July 1935 covered three full pages in the minute book plus a couple of lines on a fourth. The above extract is part of page 178 and all of page 179.

The location of the boiler house door is indicated by the lighter bricks below the bricked up window. The steps leading down into the boiler house were filled in many years ago.

felt by themselves; but all those who at any time use the room will feel grateful for the extra comfort thus secured.

The extant documentation provides no further information on this subject until April 1936 when the PCC minutes record that bills to be paid that month included one for £2.9.0. for the supply of coke. The Institute Secretary also reported that the heating pipes were still leaking in one or two places and that the doors to the boiler were falling off and required renewing or repairing but, he said, the Institute Committee had decided to defer these matters for the time being.

A year later the Secretary of the Institute Committee again reported on the problem. The Committee had met and inspected the boiler to the heating apparatus in the Institute and recommended that estimates be obtained for a new boiler and overhauling of the apparatus, the estimates to be obtained from Truswells of Newcastle, Hancock & Sons of Hanley and Mr. F. T. Hales of Hartshill. In June 1937 the following estimates for a new heating boiler were submitted:

| Truswell & Son, Newcastle | £15. 4. 0. |
| F. T. Hales, Hartshill | £16.10. 0. |

Although the higher of the two, the estimate from Mr. F. T. Hales was accepted.

Truswells came into the picture again in 1949. They had written to the Council stating that the present boiler to the heating apparatus was beyond repair and suggesting its replacement with one of similar output at a cost of £40. 6. 0. exclusive of builders' work and insulation, the old boiler to become their property for scrap.

The Council decided to seek a second opinion and received a quotation from G. S. Hall Ltd. of Hanley for £23.13.6. plus £2.15. 0. for the provision of the safety valve, thermometer, draw-off top and stoking tools In view of the fact that this total estimate was considerably lower than that of Truswells the order went to G. S Hall Ltd.

Unfortunately things did not go entirely to plan. At the 12th December 1949 meeting of the PCC it was reported that the new boiler had been on the premises for about a month but despite repeated promises it had not been installed. G. S. Hall Ltd were informed that unless steps were taken to install the boiler forthwith someone else would be employed to do it and the cost deducted from their account. This obviously had the desired effect, as the minutes of the 16th January 1950 meeting of the PCC record that "the new boiler to the Institute heating apparatus had now been installed and was working satisfactorily".

A few months later an item in the Parish Magazine about whist drives held in the Institute reminded readers that the proceeds from these events were intended "to defray the expenses of the new heating apparatus recently installed in the institute, so please do your best to come along and support a worthy cause."

Heating the Institute occupied the attention of the PCC for the final time in the late 1950s. In March 1958 it was reported that enquiries had been made about the cost of installing gas heating in the Institute and the PCC minutes record that:

Mr Tulley submitted a quotation from the West Midlands Gas Board amounting to approximately £105 and suggested that before approving the scheme the Council should decide how it was going to be financed. He reminded the Council of the constant loss on the Institute Account and stated that the loss was likely to increase during the coming year since the Saturday evening dance club which had provided the main source of income had now ceased to function.

At first the Council decided to put off taking any action, but in December of that year the Vicar informed the Council that trouble was continually being experienced with the boiler and heating apparatus at the Institute and complaints had been received from the house next door about fumes and smoke. Mr. Tulley suggested that, if it would be an expensive matter to put the present apparatus in order, the Council might consider the installation of gas heating. Estimates for this had been obtained some time ago from the Gas Board and the Council decided to go ahead with having gas heating installed.

That this was the right decision is borne out by the following extracts from the Parish Magazine in 1959:

Mothers' Union

Weather conditions prevented many members from attending the New Year Party but those who braved the bitter cold wintry conditions were well rewarded with a lovely warmed room and an excellent feast of good things. The new Gas Heaters recently installed in the Institute were a real joy and blessing to all organisations using the room for their various parties.

Church Institute

Although it was only decided at the last meeting of the P.C.C., held on the 15th December [1958], to replace the old coke boiler system of heating in the Institute by Gas heaters, yet the work was completed and the heaters ready for use before Christmas, thanks to the co-operation of the Midland Gas Board. Leaders of the various organisations using the Institute are loud in their praises regarding the difference the heaters have made to the warmth and comfort of the room. The Church Council ask for the co-operation of Leaders in Charge regarding the use of the heaters and to see they are turned off before leaving the hall and only used when needed. Each heater should he turned off separately, but NOT at the mains.

The newspaper reports of the official opening in 1859 refer to a "permanent platform erected at the end of the hall," the front of which was "hung with doors enclosing a range of shelving". The doors have long since disappeared, but the stage, as we would call it, was still in place when the Newcastle Players bought the building in 1969 (see photograph opposite) and while in use by the Church it hosted an array of concerts and other performances, notably in the 1950s by the Hartshill Entertainers.

The question of installing stage curtains and even extending the stage arose in the early 1930s and the Institute Committee was asked to look into this in October 1933. The curtains were fitted in December of that year "at a cost of £4-17-0, the amount of Messrs. Harrison's quotation", paid for from the proceeds of a collection which Mrs Dawson made among her friends and which brought in a total of £5.

Nothing appears to have been done about extending the stage at that time,

A view inside the building at the time the Newcastle Players moved in at the end of 1969. The stage is still in place and the fireplace can just be seen on the left of the picture, partially obscured by scenery flats. Note also the gas heater on the wall above

Photograph by Paul Tunstill

although it was suggested that the front of the stage be covered with plywood which Mr Barraclough offered to do.

In June 1937 the PCC asked the Institute Committee reconsider extending the stage for the Sunday School Concert. This time it was agreed to carry out the work. The cost was £4.10. 0.

As far as I am aware no further work was done on the stage until 1949, the year that The Hartshill Parish Church Entertainers came into existence. Edgar Evans, the driving force behind The Entertainers, reported to the PCC meeting on Monday 21st November that "the scenery to the Institute stage" – whatever that means – was in a bad condition and asked if it could be reconstructed in beaverboard*. He also suggested that a beaverboard pelmet be fitted above the curtains at the front of the stage. The PCC agreed to this at a cost of

* Beaverboard is a light wood-like building material, formed of wood fibre compressed into sheets. The name was originally a trademark.

approximately £3 for the reconstruction of the scenery and £24 for the pelmet.

Edgar Evans drew the PCC's attention to the stage again in 1951 when he pointed out that a crack had recently appeared over the door opening leading from the stage to the kitchen. He suggested that the partition walls be removed, the stage extended to include the present kitchen, and a new kitchen and lavatories built. The Council asked the Vicar to contact the National Coal Board about the possibility of the crack being caused by mining subsidence and suggested that a Committee already appointed to consider proposed alterations at St. Stephen's should look into the feasibility of extending the stage as proposed by Mr Evans, but nothing further appears to have been done about this.

In addition to expenditure on alterations, repairs and, from time to time, equipment such as crockery and furniture (tables and chairs), the Institute also incurred regular outgoings for gas, electricity and other fuel such as coke, plus the caretaker's wages. Sometimes these were covered in the charges for specific events which, as mentioned on page 48, in 1931 included 2/6 for the caretaker plus 6d per hour after 11 p.m. But the caretaker also received a regular wage in addition to this.

In 1933 the caretaker made a claim for extra payment for work done while the Institute was being renovated but this was rejected and the PCC resolved that "the scrubbing of chairs and other furniture" be incorporated in the caretaker's agreement. A couple of years later the PCC decided to reduce the caretaker's wages from ten shillings per week to five shillings per week during the summer, as the Institute would only be used for two nights a week. The caretaker, though, would not accept this and promptly resigned, leaving the building without a caretaker.

As an interim solution until a new caretaker was appointed arrangements were made for someone to open the Institute when required at a payment of one shilling each time it was used. In October 1935 Mr Brookes of Hartshill Road was appointed caretaker of the Institute and one of the first requests he received was "that the Institute must be kept warmer in the future". In fact Mr Brookes resigned a year later and was replaced by Mr Stanton, also of Hartshill Road. These gentlemen were presumably paid less than the unnamed caretaker who had resigned in 1935, because in May 1940 the PCC agreed to increase the caretaker's wages to ten shillings a week "owing to the increased use of the Institute". This was, of course, only a part-time job, as evidenced by the PCC's reference in 1950 to the need to employ someone full-time to cope with the possible use of the Institute for school meals (see page 50).

Although the Parochial Church Council was ultimately responsible for the

Institute, the actual running of it was in the hands of the Institute Committee. The PCC minutes record that in 1933 this committee comprised:

> Mrs. Sneyd, Miss Dawson, Miss Smith and all the Wardens – Mr. Boulton, Mrs. F Hyde

The following year the Institute Committee was expanded, as the following extract from the PCC minutes shows:

> Proposed by Mr. B. Hales and seconded by Mr. Barraclough that this Committee includes one representative of each of the Parochial organisations. This was carried and the following were elected:-
> Mrs. Sneyd, Miss Dawson, Messrs. Beckett, Boulton, Hyde, Warburton, Miss Dobell and Miss Smith and the Wardens of the Parish Church, with the addition of a representative from the 21st City of Stoke-on-Trent Boy Scouts to be nominated by Mr. B. Hales.

Edgar Evans was first elected to the Institute Committee in 1935. In 1937 Mr T. Thompson was proposed as Institute Secretary which he accepted "temporarily". I have not been able to determine how long he actually served in that capacity, but he was certainly still doing the job five years later.

Documents that I have had access to indicate that there were times when the Institute's income exceeded its expenditure, but in later years this was definitely not the case and every year from 1954 to 1965 a deficit – ranging from nine shillings and seven pence in 1956 to £135.16.10 the following year – was transferred to the Church account. There are no figures for 1966 onwards which suggests that the Institute was no longer in use by the Church.

9. Now The Newcastle Players Theatre Workshop

The Newcastle Players first came into existence in 1934. For the first eleven years or so we performed in various venues and rehearsed in different premises, some rented, others provided by friends and relations of members, all in or around Newcastle-under-Lyme. In 1945 the search for a home of our own began in earnest and this is described in my book *Founded 1934 – The Story of the Newcastle Players.*

For the first twenty or so years of our existence we hired our sets, but in 1959 we decided to purchase a basic stock flats and to establish a scenery building section. Initially we rented premises in Clough Street, Hanley which was handy for the Mitchell Memorial Theatre but hardly ideal. The space was so limited that, if somebody wanted to come in from the street while others were working on a flat supported on trestles, the flat had to be turned on its side to allow room for the door to open. This problem was solved, if that is the right word, when the owners of the building announced that it was to be demolished to make way for developments in Clough Street.

Towards the end of 1966 we found more spacious accommodation in a disused chapel in Wolstanton and we moved there in February 1967. Our tenancy did not last very long, however, because a disagreement with the owner forced us to look elsewhere for new premises suitable for building and storing scenery.

In May 1969 our then President, John Barstow, noticed that the hall in Hartshill, where he and his wife Lulu had held their wedding reception in 1927, appeared to be unused, so he decided to investigate.

That was, of course, the Hartshill Church Institute at 287 Hartshill Road, Stoke. John called on the Vicar who told him that the property was indeed for sale and suggested that he go and see the solicitors in Stoke who were handling matters on behalf of the Church Commissioners. John did this. He also inspected the building and, although there were apparently a few parts of the roof which let in water, this was not considered serious. The building's facilities were excellent with sufficient floor area and headroom to assemble the sets for our productions exactly as they would be erected on the stage of the Mitchell Memorial Theatre. He reported to the Newcastle Players Executive Committee that he had been given to understand that if we made an offer of £500 for this freehold property subject to all conditions it was likely that it would be accepted. The committee endorsed the proposal and decided that we should go ahead and buy it.

The conveyance transferring the ownership from the Lichfield Diocesan Trust to the Newcastle Players was made on Monday, 24th November 1969.

The signatories for the Diocesan Trust were The Reverend Frank William Hickling, Leonard Tulley and Sydney Woodcock – the Vicar and Church-wardens of the Parish of Hartshill.

For the Newcastle Players the signatories were John Frederick Barstow, Frederick Adolph Tunstill, William Harold Stevens and Thomas Arthur Dennis Connelley – the society's President, Secretary, Treasurer and Vice-President respectively. Or at least, those are the names as recorded on the legal document. The correct spelling of the Vice-President's last two names was Denis Connelly. F. A. Tunstill's first names were recorded correctly, although he was always known as Peter.

The Church's signatures were witnessed by L. Beardmore, Area Chief Storekeeper, of Hartshill and the other signatures by R. W. Stevens, Articled Clerk with Moxons, Solicitors, Hanley. It is worth mentioning that Newcastle Players member Richard Stevens was admitted as a solicitor a few months later. After spending time in the legal department of Rolls-Royce and as a solicitor in private practice, he went on to become a District Judge and was awarded an OBE in 2002 for his services to the modernisation of the court service. He now lives in retirement in Spain.

After having formally taken possession of the building, which we renamed "Newcastle Players Theatre Workshop", we moved our belongings from Wolstanton to Hartshill and started to deal with the necessary repair work which was expected to cost £300. We would, however, be saving £130 a year by giving up the Wolstanton premises.

At the 1970 Annual General Meeting Mary Blakeman said that the Victoria Theatre had made inquiries some time previously but that they had turned it down on an offer of £2,000 so she felt that we had really had a bargain. Another member asked whether we were likely to get heavy repeating repair bills. The President replied that vandals had got some of the lead off the roof before we took over the premises but that generally speaking, now that we had the place, he did not feel that we should have more than the normal risks.

The first set we built in the new workshop was for *Midsummer Mink*, a comedy by Peter Coke, which we presented at the Mitchell Memorial Theatre from Tuesday to Saturday, 7th to 11th April 1970. Regrettably we have no photographs of that production. In fact we did not start photographing sets for

Moving in from our previous workshop in 1969. The staircase being lifted off the lorry – and in those days we used an open lorry to transport sets – has been used in many Newcastle Players productions over the years (see pages 122 and 123 for example). The building on the right is No. 285 Hartshill Road. I cannot remember the name of the lorry driver but the identifiable Newcastle Players members in the photograph are (from left to right): Peter Tunstill, Bob West and myself (extreme right).
Photograph by Paul Tunstill

our records until many years later. The first photographs from this time I have been able to find that give any idea of what the set as a whole looked like are from our 1980 production of *Wait Until Dark* by Frederick Knott (see page 122).

The main reason for buying the workshop was to have a place of our own where we could build and store sets.

A rectangular set completely filling the available space on the stage of the Mitchell Memorial Theatre (see drawing opposite) would measure 28 feet wide (8.5 metres) by 17 feet deep (5.2 metres). In practice sets are not perfectly rectangular but trapezium-shaped (wider at the front than the back) and we don't use the full depth of the stage, because we usually have to allow room behind the set for entrances and exits or a view through a window or windows. However, we do require at least the full amount of floor space to pre-erect the set in.

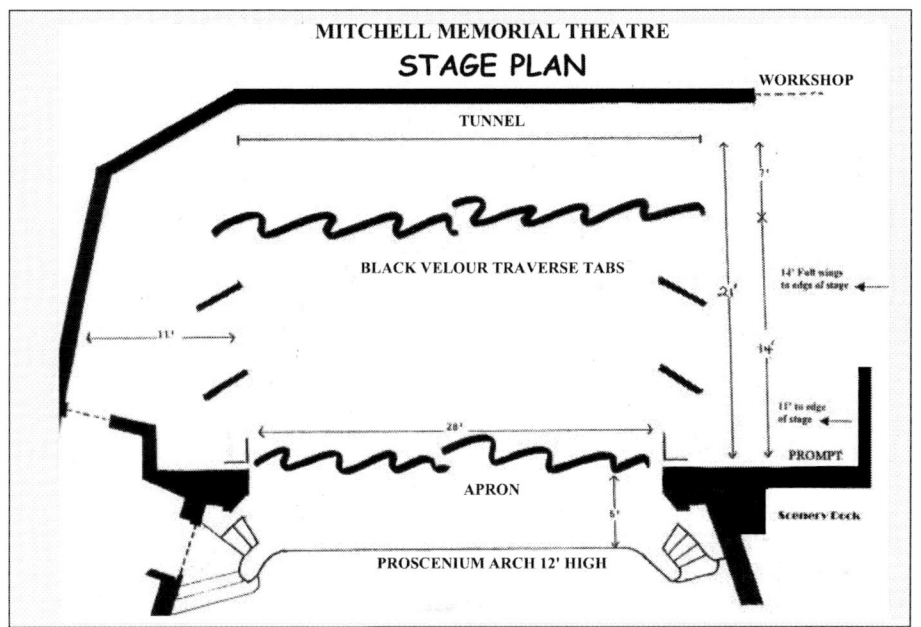

STAGE PLAN

WORKSHOP

TUNNEL

BLACK VELOUR TRAVERSE TABS

14' Felt wings
to edge of stage

21'

11'

14'

11' to edge
of stage

PROMPT

28'

APRON

Scenery Dock

5'

PROSCENIUM ARCH 12' HIGH

The flats we use are 14 feet high (4.26 metres) so we need at least that amount of headroom. In practice, though, we need rather more than that for two reasons: (a) to turn a 14 foot by 6 foot (4.26 x 1.8 m) flat onto its side, you have to take into account that measures about 15½ feet (4.7 m) across the diagonal; (b) we sometimes build at least part of the set on a rostrum, so even more headroom is needed.

The workshop fulfils both of these requirements admirably. In fact at one time we thought we had rather too much headroom, as all the warmth generated by the heating system was going up into the lantern, leaving the atmosphere at floor level rather chilly.

However, in the early years at least we used the workshop for a variety other purposes: rehearsals, jumble sales, play-readings, parties, lectures and so on.

One of the first such events was a very successful jumble sale in May 1970 which raised over £21. This was used to equip the kitchen. A second jumble sale was held four months later but there is no record of how much was raised on that occasion. Others followed at intervals to raise money for various purposes. In June 1973 it was to help finance the evening of one-act plays we put on for two nights at The Mitch for "an invited audience". In other words tickets were free!

A jumble sale in 1981 raised £160 for the Theatre Workshop Restoration Appeal Fund (see Chapter 10). The last jumble sale at the workshop was on Saturday, 16 May 1992. It raised £113.61.

Rehearsals were held quite frequently in the workshop in the 1970s and 1980s, sometimes on weekday evenings – but not Monday, when the set-building team was in action and more often on Sunday afternoons. The advantage of rehearsing at the workshop was that the cast got used to the layout of the set at an early stage, albeit without the proper furniture: a settee would be represented by three chairs side by side and tables were seldom, if ever, the right size and shape. On the other hand, the producer, prompter and other support staff had to sit virtually in the middle of the action (see photograph opposite), for on the Mitch stage (as the drawing on the previous page shows) there is potentially another three feet between the front edge of the set and the curtain line plus another five feet of apron which may also be used. Eventually, as it became more and more difficult for the set-building to team to clear their equipment out of the acting area to make way for the actors, rehearsals at the workshop were abandoned.

One slightly amusing anecdote comes to mind in connection with rehearsals. It had to be pointed out to cast members new to the workshop that it was not the cleanest of places to rehearse in and turning up in their best clothes was not recommended. However, it was an ill-advised actor who had the temerity to query why only the side of the set visible to the audience was painted while the poor old cast had to look at bare wood while waiting for their entrances. The next time he arrived at the workshop he was greeted by a pot of paint, a paintbrush and a note saying (after deletion of one or two adjectives): "If you want the other side painted, do it yourself."

Social events at the workshop ranged from beetle drives and parties to play-readings plus the odd lecture or demonstration.

One of these events was announced in the Bulletin* with reference to "the mind boggling 'beetle-drive' which was so popular last year and which nearly gave so many a coronary with all the excitement!" However, the beetle drive on Friday, 6th September 1985 generated excitement – if that's the right word – of a different kind. When three of our members went to their cars afterwards, they found that vandals had broken their aerials off and two of them were at Stoke police station until the early hours of Saturday morning! On being told where the incident had occurred, the policeman dealing with the incident

* For the benefit of readers who are not members of the Newcastle Players I should explain that the Bulletin is the members' newsletter published about ten times per year.

John Talbot and Ann McArdle rehearsing a scene from "The Heiress" at the workshop in 1993. Note the spiral staircase just over John's right shoulder and the wooden chairs in place of a settee. Producer Humphrey Gawthrop and prompter Vida Stevens are sitting practically in the middle of the action.

remarked: "Well, what d'you expect. That's right on the boundary of the Stoke and Newcastle gangs' territory. It's where they meet for a punch-up and if there's nothing going on they just break a few windows or damage a car or two!"

And we think gang culture is a 21st Century phenomenon!

On a pleasanter note, three months later there was a party advertised in the Bulletin as shown overleaf but also in the following terms:

The Next Event .....

Christmas Party

ON - FRIDAY DEC. 6th 1985 AT THE WORKSHOP

Please try to keep the date free, as this promises to be a super evening. Please also ring Mary Price on S.O.T. 617055 if you are able to come – it will help us provide enough food! We are hoping that the Workshop will again be

Newcastle Players

Christmas Party * Christmas Party *

ON - FRIDAY DEC. 6th 1985

AT - THE WORKSHOP

BAR, BUFFET AND ———— PANTOMIME!

BAR OPENS AT 8.00 P.M.   BUFFET AT 8.30 P.M.
************************   ********************

TICKETS £1.50

'transformed' to suit the occasion and time of the year, BUT, as many of you know already, please come suitably dressed for the Workshop. Some of our newer members may not be familiar with the inside, so for their benefit:-

Ladies: Please do not come in your most expensive 'posh frock'.

Gents: Likewise (!?!)

This was in fact the culmination of a very full 1985 calendar for the Newcastle Players as the panel on page opposite shows. Not everything took place at the workshop, but six of the events did.

The event at The Workshop on Friday 31st May – *The Players Entertain Themselves* – was a great success. The Bulletin reported what it described as "a fun evening" as follows:

The Social Evening . . . . lived up to the title of the evening – the Players certainly did 'entertain themselves'. The evening was, enjoyed by almost 50 members and guests and for those who were unable to come along, I know you will be interested to know what went on!

Prue Winnett played the flute, accompanied by John Turner on his guitar; Carol Langton read 'Some of me poems' by Pam Ayres; Geoff Price entertained us with his bongos etc; Mary Blakeman gave us a funny tale she had inherited from the late John Barstow; John Turner told us a joke; Jim Ward kept on telling us jokes; Bruce Haycock serenaded us; Lea Nicholson read and played for us; Philip Eardley did a spot of magic; Sue Henderson & Katja Yorke did a 'comic strip'; and the whole evening ended with our compere, Jim, involving other 'game-for-a-laf' members in a musical quiz game.

Geoff Lawrence, the guest speaker on Friday, 14th June 1985, was BBC Radio Stoke's Station Manager at the time. He gave a very interesting talk

The Newcastle Players' calendar of events planned for 1985.

about the work of the local radio station which, in the words of the Bulletin, "stimulated some varied comments and discussions". The Bulletin also reported that the workshop "was 'transformed' for a few hours into a 'cabaret style' layout allowing for a projector and screen to be erected" and it added thanks to Philip Eardley and the backstage team who had set it up and took it all down afterwards to get ready for the *Summer Evening's Entertainment* to be staged at the Mitch the following month.

Another speaker at the workshop was Jessie Shaw, the doyenne of the mobile stage make-up teams that provided a service for all the local operatic groups. Unlike the latter, members of the Newcastle Players do their own make-up. What Jessie Shaw did was to show us how to do some of the more complicated techniques. Taking three of our members – Wendy Lowe, Paul Godfrey and Sonny Diego – as models she demonstrated how to make them look young, old and very old.

Play-readings ranged from one-act plays – a sort of audition giving newer members an opportunity to show what they were capable of – up to a very full read performance of Arnold Ridley's *The Ghost Train* complete with all the sound and lighting effects called for in the script. This was produced by Vida

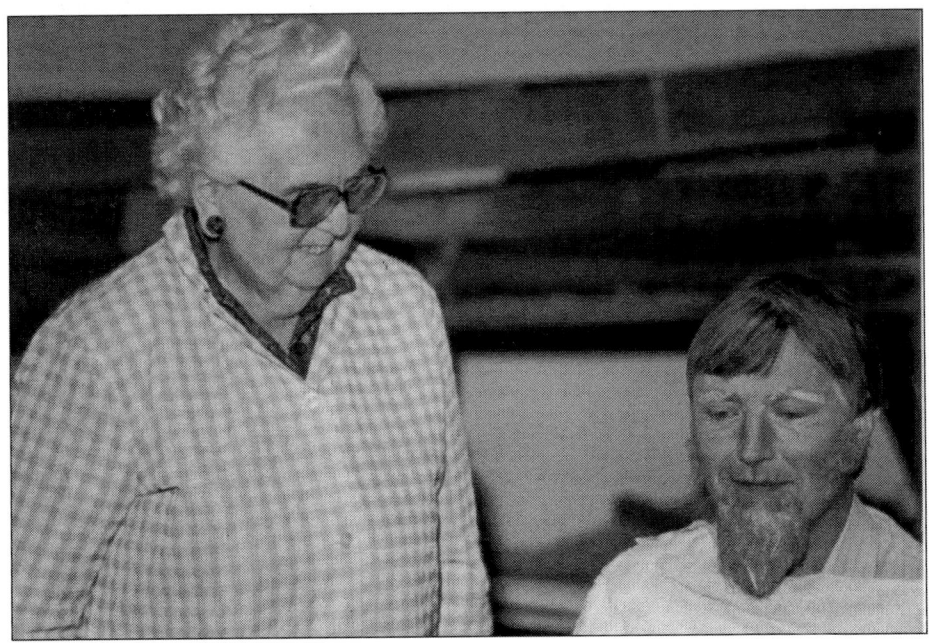

Make-up expert Jessie Shaw with Paul Godfrey transformed into an old man during a demonstration of make-up techniques at the workshop in June 1986.

Stevens and proved a very nostalgic evening for our oldest members as *The Ghost Train* was the very first play to be presented by the Newcastle Players back in 1935. It was to be 2005 before we staged a full revival of the play at the Mitchell Memorial Theatre.

The last social event held at the workshop was another Christmas party on Friday, 11th December 1987. Almost sixty people attended. The Bulletin recorded "Thanks . . . . to the GP (General Purpose) and social committees for organising it and decorating the workshop, Helen Foy who provided all the lovely food and the performers themselves."

Over the years the local media has taken an interest in our workshop from time to time. *The Sentinel* for example devoted nearly a whole page to what it called the "Old Masters" on the set-building team in its issue of Wednesday, 19th April 1995 (see opposite page).

One of the "Old Masters" was Pat Mason who, as I describe in the next chapter, masterminded our Lottery bid. In this connection BBC Radio Stoke devoted an hour-long programme (with breaks for music, news bulletins and

Old masters in the art of DIY

THEIR combined ages may be 220, but Ben, Pat and Alan are pensioners with a purpose.

When the curtain goes up on any Newcastle Players production, it's their handiwork that gives an amateur show the West End look.

The company — 60 years old last year — haven't hired scenery for 35 years, relying on volunteers like Ben, Pat and Alan to create sets to order in their own workshop at Hartshill.

And it's a tribute to their diligence and skill that Newcastle Players' stage sets are the envy of the local theatre scene. "They always look right for the play," says spokesman Jonathan Ferneyhough.

"It is acknowledged that our scenery tends to stay in one place, that doors don't stick and so on. There's a professional look to our productions and it's all thanks to our unpaid pensioners."

BY ALAN COOKMAN

Under the supervision of workshop manager John Hough, retired businessman Ben Devall (84) and his friends Pat Mason and Alan Davies, both aged 68, are this week putting the finishing touches to the set for the Patrick Cargill comedy "Don't Misunderstand Me," which opens at the Mitchell Memorial Theatre, Hanley on Monday.

"The producer tells John what he wants, and John tells the producer what he can have," says Jonathan. "Then it's all down to Ben, Pat and Alan."

And their latest project calls for a wallpapered sitting room, part of a tiled kitchen and a colourful garden visible through the windows.

The company bought their own "flats" — 14ft tall scenery boards — in 1960 and converted premises in Clough Street, Hanley into a store-room and workshop.

"The sets were purpose-built and painted in the workshop and carried, piece by piece, the 300 yards to the Mitchell Memorial Theatre," says Pat, a retired Wedgwood works director.

"But this did tend to cause traffic jams, and it was fraught with hazards in bad weather. Strong winds were lethal — the flats were made of canvas and acted like sails when hit by fierce gusts."

In November 1969, the Players bought the former church hall at Hartshill. "The old building was badly in need of structural repairs and the Vicar thought it was preferable for us to have it than

see it turned into a nightclub or replaced by a supermarket," says Pat.

Supported by a "Buy a Brick" scheme, volunteers led by stalwarts Bill Stevens, Arthur Gennery and Pat set about restoring the building, and since 1970 a succession of dedicated set builders and decorators have toiled in the workshop where Pat, Ben and Alan now spend their Monday evenings (putting in many extra hours when a production is imminent).

In an incident worthy of a Whitehall farce, the pensioners once brought Hartshill to a stand-

- **Above: From left: Pat, Alan and Ben at work**

Left: Ben applies his brush to a bush on the scenery

still after inadvertently leaving a gas heater on in the empty workshop for several weeks.

"The light had gone out and the building filled with gas," Pat recalls. "Roads were closed and houses evacuated as the building was cleared of gas. The emergency services not amused, nor were neighbouring householders who had to stand around all night in their pyjamas.

"A Gas Board man said if the gas had ignited, the building would have gone up and taken most of Hartshill with it."

- **"Don't Misunderstand Me" is at the Mitchell Memorial Theatre, April 24-28 at 7.30pm. Tel 01782 617055.**

The above article featuring Pat Mason, Alan Davies and Ben Devall at the workshop appeared in The Sentinel of Wednesday, 19th April 1995.

Reproduced by courtesy of Staffordshire Sentinel News & Media

so on) to a live visit to the workshop by Barbara Adams on Wednesday, 13th November 1996 hosted by Pat.

More recently John Hough was interviewed at the workshop by BBC Radio Stoke reporter – and Newcastle Players member – Helen Thomas on Friday, 19th May 2006 and Becky Wood interviewed me about our 150th Anniversary Open Evening on Friday, 9th January 2009.

There are recordings of all three interviews in our archives.

10. Fabric and Finance since 1969

It may have only cost the Newcastle Players £500 to buy the Hartshill Church Institute in 1969, but since then, as The Newcastle Players Theatre Workshop, it has cost many thousands of pounds to run and maintain. Not only have there been regular outgoings on such things as gas, electricity, water, council tax and insurance, but other major items of expenditure have been incurred on repairs and refurbishment with the added complication of the setting up of the Hartshill Conservation Area in 1976, designation of the workshop as a Grade II Listed Building in 1993 and our failed Lottery bid later in the 1990s.

The main reason for our disagreement with the owner of the property which we had rented in Wolstanton and our decision to move out was his refusal to pay the rates to Newcastle Borough Council, although this was his responsibility according to the rental contract. He said he had discovered that cultural organisations got a rates rebate, so it was up to the Newcastle Players to pay the rates and claim the rebate. However, he was not prepared to reduce our rent to compensate for this.

On taking up occupancy of the former Church Institute we asked the City of Stoke-on-Trent Rates Department for details of how to apply for reduced rates on account of the society's cultural activities. It took some months to sort this out. Our initial application for a rent rebate was turned down, because we were not registered with the Charity Commission and the Charity Commission told us that our constitution did not conform to the model laid down by the British Drama League. The main difference concerned the aims of the society. The solution was to revise our constitution as required. The revised constitution was submitted to the 1971 Annual General Meeting and approved. Following this action the society was officially registered with the Charity Commission (Registered Charity No. 501135) in October 1971.

The question of heating the workshop has reared its ugly head from time to time just as it did throughout the building's history as the Hartshill Working Men's Institution and the Hartshill Church Institute – and as it does to the present day. A few months after we moved in Vice-President Bill Stevens managed to acquire seven tubular heaters at a cost of ten shillings each and, the Executive Committee minutes record, "he was congratulated by the President for his astuteness in obtaining such an excellent bargain." At about the same time Enid Tunstill was able to obtain a water heater for the workshop for five pounds.

Maybe the tubular heaters were not such a bargain after all, for in February 1974 the Executive Committee investigated the cost of night-storage heaters. It concluded that these would be too expensive so it went for an alternative solution: two gas heaters costing £230.23 plus £61 for new service pipes. These were duly installed and the August 1974 Bulletin reported this with the comment that, "if any of the scenery painters were standing around with a brush in their hands, at least they could now do so in some warmth and comfort!!"

The roof has been another recurring problem. This first arose in the spring of 1976 when gales caused some leaking. Quotations were obtained from Area Roofing for £280 and from Robert Jackson for £550, the former being accepted, but it took several months for the job to be completed to our satisfaction.

Operation "Clean-Up"

At about the same time there was some discussion about tidying up the workshop so that we could make more use of it in an attempt to offset the cost of room hire for committee meetings, rehearsals and social events. We established the code name "Clean-Up" for this operation. The President, John Barstow, offered to tile the toilet and added that, if we could find some willing members of the society to help, we could make the toilet and the kitchen a little more inviting.

It was several months before this work could get under way, because we realised that some serious remedial action had to be taken first to correct damp and dry rot. This involved replacing the guttering and downspouts on the outside of the building with new ones, replastering the kitchen and toilet walls and removing all the timber affected by dry rot – namely the kitchen and toilet floor and the stage – to prevent it spreading to the rest of the building.

The stage was removed by members of the Newcastle Players in February 1977 and the rest of the work including replacing the joists and floorboards in the kitchen, was done at a cost of £417.00 plus VAT by local building contractor C. H. Tunstill (known as Nobby), the brother of our then Secretary F. A. Tunstill (known as Peter).

This and previous expenditure on the workshop was eating into the financial reserves we had built up through surpluses on our productions, so we sought assistance from West Midlands Arts whose reply, in its own word, was "discouraging":

> West Midlands Arts, the regional arts association, has very limited funds and cannot normally consider giving capital grants for buildings or equipment. In addition, we are not normally able to contribute directly to wholly amateur theatre activities.

The Hartshill Conservation Area

In 1977 the area surrounding and including the workshop was officially designated the Hartshill Conservation Area and we were informed by the City of Stoke-on-Trent's Director of Environmental Services that:

> No part of any building within the Conservation Area shall be treated with any form of cement rendering or stone cladding including imitation stonework cladding without the prior consent of the Local Planning Authority.

> No external brickwork of any building within the Conservation Area shall be painted without the prior consent of the Local Planning Authority.

The impact of the creation of the conservation area was brought home to us in April 1980 by the letter we received from the Director of Environmental Services, which is reproduced overleaf. This was the start of a period of intense activity aimed at renovating the workshop. Although the initial letter only referred to woodwork, further investigation by the President's brother, Mr F E Stevens, who was a registered and incorporated architect and surveyor, and also by a Mr Hollins of the County Architect's Department revealed a wider range of problems. Then at the end of the year dry rot became an issue again. This was investigated by Rentokil's Woodworm & Dry Rot Division which submitted a very comprehensive report and quoted a figure of £2,900 to put the matter right.

At that stage it was felt that £5,000 would be necessary to put the workshop in order. However, to prevent any further abortive discussion on this very important subject, as the Executive Committee minutes put it, an Ad Hoc Committee was set up consisting of Pat Mason, Paul Godfrey, Pat Sunderland and George Hurlstone. Their brief was to discuss all aspects of the problem including exploring the possibility of disposing of the building altogether and either renting or buying an alternative. They were also to discuss ways of encouraging our existing members to raise the sum it was thought was required.

Alongside this approaches were made to various bodies asking for

City of Stoke-on-Trent

John Shryane, M.R.T.P.I., R.I.B.A., F.R.S.A.
Director of Environmental Services

Mr F A Tunstill
Blithe Cottage
Tavistock Crescent
NEWCASTLE
Staffordshire ST5 3NW

P.O. Box 207
Unity House
Hanley
Stoke-on-Trent ST1 4QL

Telephone Extn 2292
Stoke-on-Trent 29611 (STD Code 0782)

Your ref   Our ref PL/MGD/AJB (Mr M G Downs)   Date   25 April 1980

Dear Sir

Premises of The Newcastle Players,
287 Hartshill Road, Hartshill.

I understand that you are the Secretary of the Newcastle Players who
occupy the above building.

This property, as you will be aware, lies within the Hartshill Conservation
Area, which is a protected area under several pieces of environmental
legislation.

It has recently been brought to my attention that the woodwork of 287
Hartshill Road is currently in a rather poor state of repair. My
assistant has recently visited the site and is of the opinion that if
the external woodwork of the property is not satisfactorily restored
and repainted in the near future, then wood rot will become chronic and
very expensive to remedy.

I would therefore urge you on behalf of the Newcastle Players to take
the necessary action to preserve this building at an early stage, and
thereby maintain the quality of the environment in the Conservation
Area and avoid storing up more serious and costly problems for the
future.

Yours faithfully

John Shryane

Director   20

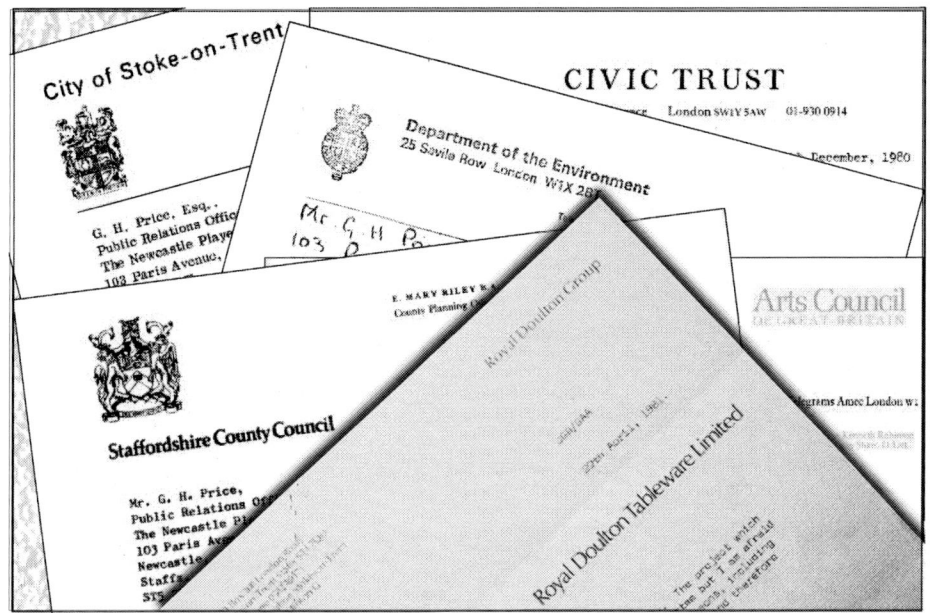

A selection of the letters we received in response to our requests for financial assistance.

financial assistance – with varying degrees of success but not amounting to very much in the way of money.

All these problems were aired and discussed in great detail at our Annual General Meeting in February 1981 and the various suggestions made were handed over to the Ad Hoc Committee for consideration. In July 1981 an Extraordinary General Meeting was held and I see from the minutes that I gave "a superb verbal and slide presentation giving a full description of the problems at the workshop with details of the conservation order and the results of our requests for grants and financial assistance." A few of the pictures I showed are reproduced on the next four pages. More importantly Ad Hoc Committee member Paul Godfrey "gave full details of what the committee had done over the last few months and what the society as a whole needed to do now with regard to fundraising."

The outcome of this was that a £10,000 appeal was launched and various fund-raising activities were initiated. These included:

- A Buy-a-Brick Campaign

- The presentation of an extra play in August 1981 (*How the Other Half Loves* by Alan Ayckbourn)

The external woodwork in a poor state of repair reported by the assistant to Stoke-on-Trent's Director of Environmental Services.

Some of the external brickwork was also in a poor state and needed replacing, but it had to be done with bricks of the right era.

Internally there was quite a bit of damage to the underside of the roof . . .

. . . and dry rot, such as here in one of the beams supporting the balcony; the handrail to the spiral staircase can be seen in the left half of the picture.

At the end of his 180-mile sponsored cycle ride from Newcastle-on-Tyne Bruce Haycock was welcomed by our President Bill Stevens and the Mayor of Newcastle-under-Lyme, Councillor Vic Finnemore as Carnival Queen Pam Kelly looked on.

- A sponsored cycle ride from Newcastle-on-Tyne to Newcastle-under-Lyme by Bruce Haycock supported by a team led by Philip Eardley

- A jumble sale, a coffee evening, a bring & buy sale, quiz, china sale, cheese and wine evening and so on.

Repair work started soon after the Extraordinary General Meeting supervised by the Ad Hoc Committee with professional advice from architect David Riley. Rentokil's work was finished at the beginning of October, but the replacement of other woodwork and replastering was put on hold until after the autumn play (*My Three Angels* – see picture opposite).

Bricks proved to be something of a stumbling block (please excuse the pun). Under the terms of the Conservation Area we were required to replace any that had suffered deterioration with matching bricks from the same (Victorian) era, but we had been assured that the County Architect's department in Stafford kept stocks of such things. This contact proved useless, but after several months our architect located a builder who was demolishing some houses of the right period in Burslem and who said that we could have as many bricks as we wanted provided we transported them off his site.

A scene from our 1981 production of "My Three Angels" with (from left to right) Bob West, Reg Williams, Paul Godfrey and John Talbot.

Photograph by Paul Tunstill

Heating was also dealt with by the Ad Hoc Committee and in the autumn of 1982 an industrial heater was installed. At the time of writing it is still there, but it is giving signs of coming to the end of its useful life.

By the time of our 1983 Annual General Meeting the President, Bill Stevens, was able to report that the major part of the restoration work had been successfully completed. This had been possible due to grants from the City of Stoke-on-Trent and the Staffordshire Councils, the fund-raising efforts by the Players themselves, but above all, to the generosity of the Society's patrons, without whose help and support the project would have proved extremely difficult.

The Conservation Order on the building had created some considerable difficulties, he said, but these had been overcome and the standard of work had been praised by Mr John Shryane, the City of Stoke-on-Trent's Director of Environmental Services. In a letter to the Society he not only congratulated the Newcastle Players on the success of the project but also added:

The building has been carefully restored and is now a credit to the Hartshill Conservation area.

Later that year two alterations to the interior of the building were considered, one we proceeded with and one we rejected:

1. As already mentioned, heating has been a recurring problem throughout the history of the building. Whereas the internal height of the building was and still is an advantage when it comes to erecting scenery, there was quite an amount of space above the height we required for practical purposes where any heat generated at floor level accumulated leaving the occupants shivering below. Our solution was to fit a suspended ceiling which created a pleasanter atmosphere in the working area.

2. The other change considered was to modify the gallery over the front entrance to the building so that it could be utilised for committee meetings. The gallery was, and still is, accessed via a cast-iron spiral staircase. Its floor is not flat but stepped so the possibility of installing a floor on one level and partitioning off the gallery with glass partitioning was investigated. This would have created a room approximately 9 ft wide by 25 ft long which could be screened off from the body of the hall with glass partitioning. After careful consideration, however, it was felt that it would take up space currently used for storage and create a room that would not be at all comfortable for a committee of twelve or so members, sometimes even more. It was agreed, therefore, to take no further action with this.

The Workshop Manager

Up until 1992 no one member was responsible for the workshop. Various people had keys to the property and it was tacitly understood that if the Executive Committee wanted an opinion on workshop matters Pat Mason was the person it turned to. Similarly, if there was a requirement to open the building for a non-key-holder, Pat was the man to contact. This was certainly the case in 1981 when, due to an oversight, the gas was left switched on but unlit for several weeks. This was discovered when local residents smelled gas and called out the gas board and the emergency services. Pat was duly summoned and, on arriving at the workshop, he found that the area had been cleared and he was told in no uncertain terms that it was up to him to unlock the doors, to go in and switch off the gas, and to wait until the official representatives were satisfied that the building was safe before locking it up again. That is a mistake that we have never repeated.

In 1992 Pat reached the age of 65 and let it be known that he wished to be relieved of his workshop responsibilities. At that point the Executive

Workshop Manager John Hough being interviewed on air at the workshop by BBC Radio Stoke journalist Helen Thomas, who was also a Newcastle Players member before she left the district to join to BBC Radio 5 .

Committee decided that it would be a good idea to nominate one person as Workshop Manager. John Hough was suggested for the job, which he has done excellently ever since. In 1995 in fact the Workshop Manager became an officer of the society alongside the President, Chairman, Vice-Chairman, Secretary, Treasurer and Public Relations Officer.

Grade II Listed Building

On 15th March 1993 the Department of National Heritage listed the Newcastle Players Theatre Workshop as a building of special architectural or historic interest, making it a Grade II Listed Building. The cottages on either side of the workshop and Hartshill Church are also listed buildings.

Grade II Listed Building status places even greater restrictions on what we can do with the building than those applicable to the conservation area. In a written reply to a parliamentary question about this in 1998 the then Minister for the Arts, Alan Howarth MP (now Baron Howarth of Newport), said: "The Planning (Listed Buildings and Conservation Areas) Act 1990 requires the owner of any listed building to obtain listed building consent for any works of demolition or for any works of alteration or extension which would affect its character as a building of special architectural or historic interest. The carrying out of such works without prior consent is a criminal offence."

Over 180 buildings in The Potteries are listed. The Heritage Number of our workshop is 67a and details of it can be found at www.thepotteries.org/listed/67a.html. The website lists not only the address but also the National Grid reference: SJ8645SE. There are photographs of our workshop (similar to those on pages 60 and 62) plus the following description:

> Former Institute opened in 1859, now in use as a theatre workshop.
> Brick with stone dressings and plain tiled roof with scalloped tiles and ridge cresting. Gable facing the street, with advanced gabled porch with paired shafts to the doorway flanked by casement windows beneath 2-centred relieving arches with embossed tiles in the apex of the arch.
> Small rose window truss are carried on corbels.

Lottery Application

In 1996 we started to examine the possibility of restoring the exterior of the building to its former glory and carrying out considerable refurbishment to the interior with a view to converting it into The Newcastle Players Theatre Centre, which would have involved extensive alterations both inside and out.

The exterior work was to involve cleaning, treating and, where possible, preserving the exterior fabric of the building, replacing the paved area at the front and reglazing the windows in keeping with their original 1850s style. The result would have been not only to enhance the appearance of our building but also to add to the appeal of the Minton Cottages on one side and the Campbell Cottages on the other.

Internally we intended to expand on the rejected plans for the gallery by enlarging and enclosing it, inserting a floor on a single level (in place of the original stepped floor) and creating a new room which would serve as our headquarters, meeting room, social room and rehearsal room. This would be accessed via a timber staircase (see drawing on page 100) to replace the existing spiral staircase.

The kitchen and toilet facilities were to be transferred to the area at the front of the building under the new room, while the existing kitchen, paint store, toilet and the boiler room beneath were to be gutted and refurbished after the floor has been lowered to the same level as the rest of building to become our workshop, tool store and small effects room.

Last but not least the floor in the main hall was to be attended to. According to the professional advice we received, the flooring was in excellent condition and the quality of the timber probably superior to flooring which could be purchased today. However, after almost a century and a half

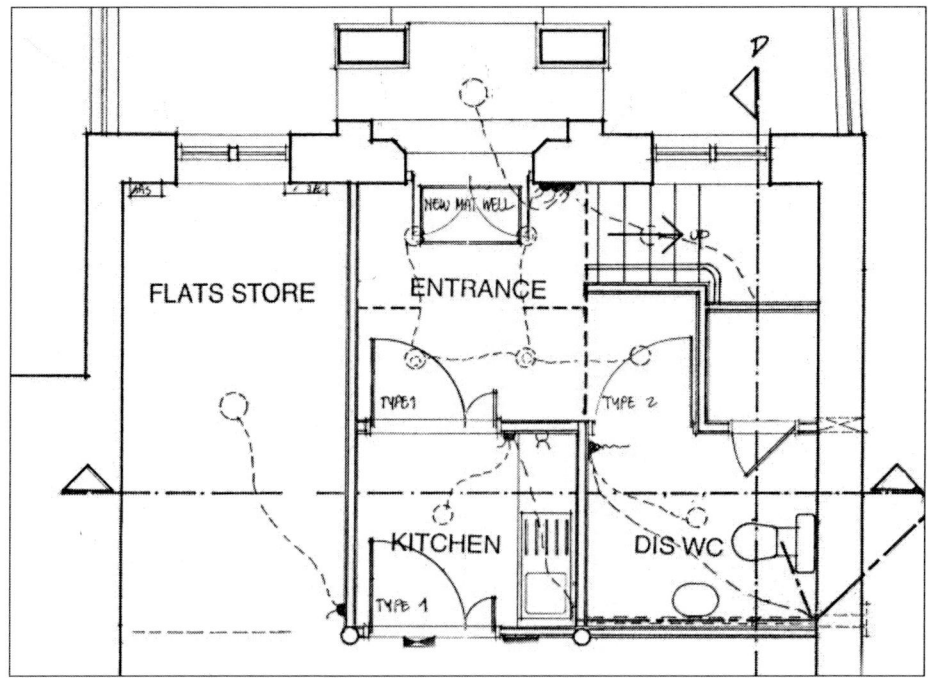

The sketches above and overleaf are extracts from the architect's drawings showing the changes we proposed to make to the entrance area of the building in plan (above) and in section (overleaf).

of use, it had developed a slope from one side to the other which created (and still creates) some problems for our set builders. This we intended to correct.

We were planning to carry out this work during our close season (April to August) in 1997 under the supervision of the architects, Anthony Blacklay and Associates of Nantwich, who had considerable experience in dealing with historical buildings.

It was, of course, going cost a considerable sum of money. To this end we submitted an application to the Arts Council of England for a grant from the National Lottery Fund. However, we were also required to provide what is known as "partnership funding". We, therefore, committed £5,000 from our own reserves as well as approaching a number of charitable trusts, the relevant local authorities and other bodies for assistance and also carrying out several special fund-raising activities with the aim of raising a further £5,000.

Our Lottery bid was masterminded by Pat Mason, who came out of retirement to take on this onerous task. Preparing the bid took longer than we had hoped, so we abandoned ideas of doing the work in 1997 and reset our sights on the summer of 1998. We were eventually in a position to submit our

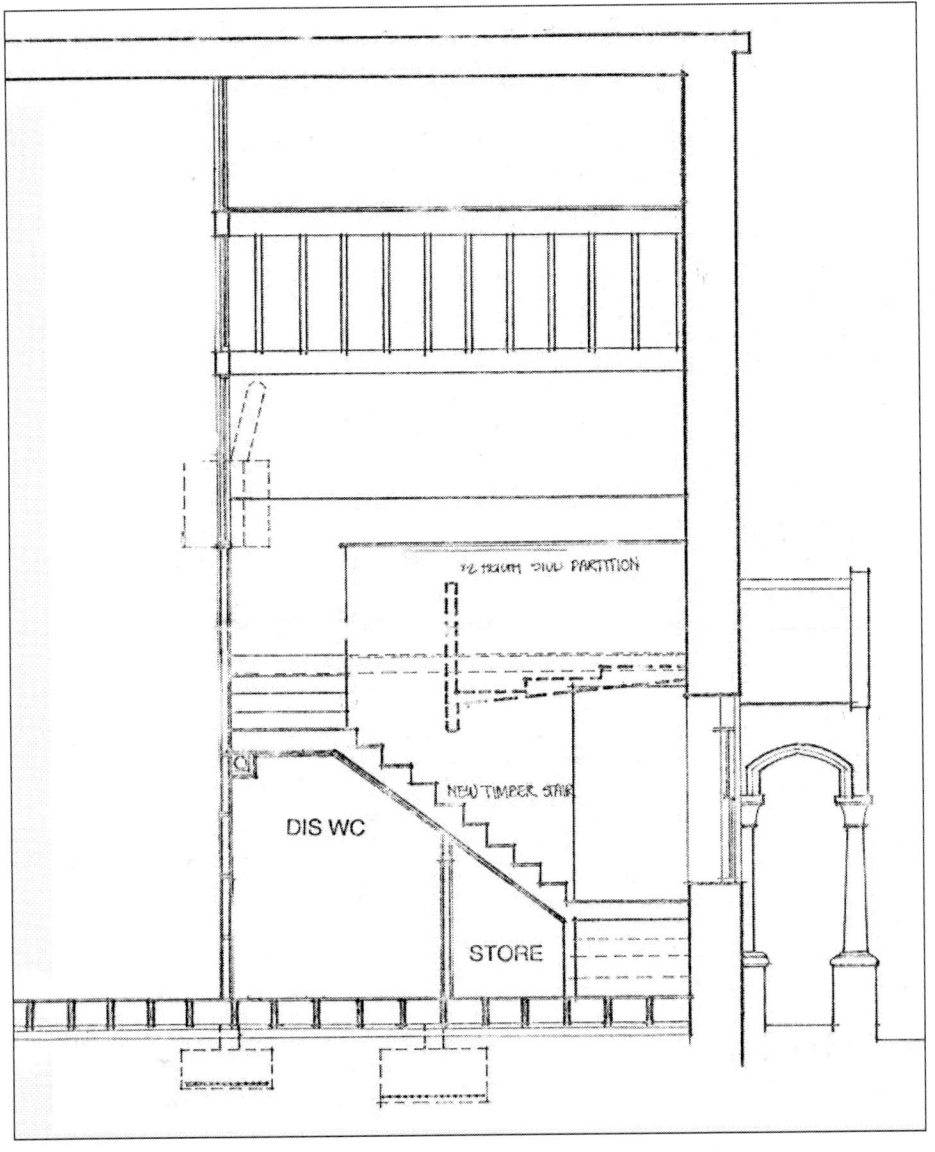

The new timber staircase to replace the existing spiral staircase can be clearly seen in the sketch above.

application in July 1997. Basically this was a twelve page form accompanied by a further fifty pages of supporting documentation. There then followed innumerable telephone calls and letters from the Arts Council requesting clarification of various points. At one stage the clarifying documentation

Architect Anthony Blacklay (left) and his assistant (second right) take a break from studying the drawings of the proposed changes to the workshop with John Hough, Jim Ward and Pat Mason to pose for the camera.

supplied was three times bigger than the original application and weighed over a kilogram. At another stage we received a two-page letter with yet more questions and a request that our reply be in the hands of the Arts Council within five days. There were times, it must be admitted, when we felt that we had overcome one hurdle only to be faced by another.

Our application was supported by a wide range of influential people connected with the theatre and in public life. They included Peter Cheeseman, Director of the New Victoria Theatre; Councillor Alan Edwards, Vice-Chair of the City of Stoke-on-Trent's Leisure & Cultural Services and Chair of the Cultural Services Sub-Committee; Councillor John P Birkin, Lord Mayor of Stoke-on-Trent; Stoke-on-Trent Councillors Tom Brennan, John Beech and Cliff Hathaway; Peter Dutton, Chairman of Stoke-on-Trent Repertory Theatre; and, last but not least, Stoke-on-Trent Central MP and Shadow Minister for the Arts Mark Fisher.

We were encouraged by one letter from West Midlands Arts which said that we had submitted a model application and requesting our permission to use it as an example to be followed by other applicants. In spite of this, though,

THE NEWCASTLE PLAYERS
FOUNDED 1934

THE NEWCASTLE PLAYERS THEATRE WORKSHOP
287 HARTSHILL ROAD,
STOKE - ON - TRENT,
STAFFORDSHIRE,
ST4 - 7NQ.

AN APPLICATION FOR LOTTERY FUNDING TO -:

THE ARTS COUNCIL OF ENGLAND
14 GREAT PETER STREET
LONDON
SW1P - 3NQ

JUNE 1997

The front cover of our lottery application document complete with the project manager, Pat Mason, standing by the car.

Photograph on the cover by John Hough

in December 1997 we received the response to our application. It contained the crucial but disappointing sentence: "The Arts Council of England has decided not to approve a grant of National Lottery funding for this project."

This meant that, after a lot of work and the expenditure of several thousand pounds on architect's and other professional fees, we were no further forward. In fact we were worse off financially than when we started.

So where did we go wrong? To obtain such funding it is necessary to satisfy eight criteria:

1. Benefit to the public (including access for disabled people)
2. Long-term effect on the organisation's financial stability
3. Amount of partnership funding
4. Quality of design and construction
5. Quality of artistic activities planned
6. Relevance to local, regional and national plans for the arts
7. Contribution of artists, craftspeople and film and video makers
8. Quality of the organisation's plans for education and marketing

We had been led to believe in our preliminary negotiations with West Midlands Arts that, in the event of an application being rejected, the reason for the rejection would be given. In the event all we were told initially was that the Arts Council felt our application "was less strong in respect of . . . the quality of design and construction".

Further discussions with West Midlands Arts eventually led us to believe that our project had not been ambitious enough. We had attempted to keep the costs within a budget of £100,000 since this would have meant our only having to find ten per cent of the cost from our own or other resources. Reading between the lines of subsequent correspondence led us to believe that the Arts Council would have preferred us to go for a much bigger project, possibly costing £150,000 or even £200,000 and requiring us to find twenty-five per cent of the cost. In other words our contribution would have had to go up from £10,000 to possibly as much £50,000, which we believed to be beyond our resources.

In view of this, plus the fact that the money available to the arts had been reduced and the number of applications had increased, we decided to abandon our plans to refurbish the workshop in a single stage with the help of National Lottery funding.

The new refurbishment project

Over the next few years repairs were carried out on an ad hoc basis whenever the need occurred and whenever available funds permitted. In 2005, however, we decided that a major effort was required and a new project was launched, as described in the following article from the Bulletin of September of that year:

A number of years ago, the society was forced to have the large front area of the workshop roof repaired and put in good order as all the nails holding the tiles were rotting and tiles kept falling off, creating leaks. This cost us over £4500 all of which had to come out of the society's limited funds.

When Newcastle Players bought the workshop, the rear of the roof was leaking and, after purchasing the property, we had not got enough money left at the time to fully repair it properly. Therefore the roof tiles were covered in felt, as a makeshift job. This has been satisfactory up until now. The felt has now started to rot and the rear part of the roof was, at the last count, leaking in three places. We have kept having temporary cheaper jobs done in the hope that this would suffice, but now the time has come to repair the roof properly. Unfortunately, due to the fact that the building is now categorised as Grade II listed, re-felting is not an option.

During the summer we continued with the ongoing process of the reorganization of the workshop recently begun to create better storage for our production materials and during this we found quite a lot of rotten areas in the floor, especially around the edges, along with the couple of places in the centre hat we knew about (the workshop team has learned to dance around these over the years). The floor has been of some concern for many years for different reasons, as it is not flat or level, which at times makes it difficult to build sets. The time, therefore, has come to also replace the floor, mainly for safety's sake and not just to make it level.

The total cost of the replacing both the roof and floor is estimated as being in the region of £11,000 to £12,000, so we are desperately in need of all your support in raising this money. Unfortunately as the society does not have the necessary funds to complete, or even start the work, so we are turning to you, our membership to help to raise the required funds.

We are asking every member, where possible, if they can make a regular monthly donation of between £5 and £10. On these donations, if you complete and sign the enclosed form, we will be able to claim Gift Aid (providing you qualify) which will in effect make your £10 monthly donation rise to £12.80. Once completed, return the whole form to John Hough who will then copy it for our records and then forward the Standing Order part of the form to your bank and hold the Gift Aid declaration part until required to claim the Gift Aid.

But this hopefully is only the start. Our aim is to fully refurbish the workshop to the standard we would ideally wish, including the provision of a rehearsal room which will in total cost in excess of £200,000.

To achieve this we are also seeking funding from as many grant providing bodies as possible to help to provide funding for the entire cost of the project, but as with all funding, you have to show that you are attempting to raise at least a proportion of the costs yourselves and by giving on a regular basis, we hope to show this. This is work that is badly overdue.

We are not kidding ourselves and know it may take some time to raise the money, but if 50 people donate £10.00 per month, within 6 to 8 months we would have enough money to do the roof, then within another 10 months enough to do the floor.

This is your hobby and your society. Without the workshop we can't build sets, without those sets we cannot put on plays to the standard we do and without plays we no longer exist. If you want to see this society continue, always producing quality entertainment, then please **give generously!!**

This was the start. Some members, but not all by any means, committed themselves to giving a regular amount of money over a certain period and quite a few fund-raising events have taken place, raising sums of various sizes. The major event was a one-night stand at The Rep in Stoke in September 2005.

Back in 1994 our friends at Stoke-on-Trent Repertory Theatre were raising money to build their new theatre in Leek Road. It was our 60th Anniversary year and, although not specifically part of our celebrations, we thought it would be appropriate to donate £1000 to the Rep's building appeal. Eleven years later, when we were looking for financial assistance, The Rep reciprocated by giving us the use of their theatre free of charge to put on an evening in aid of our Workshop Restoration Fund.

The event took the form of a gala concert entitled *The Best of Summertime* on Saturday, 9th September 2006. It played to a full house and it was also a great social occasion with over 200 people thronging the theatre foyer and bar, drinking wine and fruit juice while they chatted to their friends and acquaintances. And the whole event made a great contribution to the workshop fund. The gross takings were in excess of £2000 for which we must be grateful to the fifty or so people taking part, to everybody who bought tickets but above all to The Rep for the use of their splendid theatre.

Shortly after the gala evening work started on repairs to the roof. A few months later the woodwork on the front of the workshop was repainted to make it all look shiny and clean. At more or less the same time new street lighting was installed on the stretch of Hartshill Road from the workshop to the Noah's Ark pub. The lamp-posts are the modern tubular variety but the lamps themselves are pendants with a period (Victorian?) look and clear glass inverted pear shape globes. One of the new lamps was erected right outside the workshop where it spoils the view of the front from one angle but at least it throws light into the alleyway between the workshop and the nearest Minton cottage.

The repainted woodwork, the repaired roof and the new lamp post with its pear-shaped globe.

During the 2008 summer break – before building the set for *Cash On Delivery* – a team of members led by Workshop Manager John Hough and Chairman Rob Vaughan started cleaning and redecorating the interior of the building. The false ceiling was removed and scaffolding erected to support a temporary floor just below where the suspended ceiling was, to enable the workers to get at the top few feet of the walls and the underside of the roof. This meant, of course, that for the first time in something like twenty-five years it was now possible to see the inside of the roof in every detail. Once the upper level had been cleaned and painted the scaffolding was removed ready for the Open Evening celebrating the building's 150th Anniversary.

But that is the subject of the next chapter.

The repainted lantern, ceiling and upper walls. Spot lights have been installed to illuminate the interior of the lantern and fans to drive the accumulated warmth from the main heater back down to floor level.

11. 150 Years Old and The Show Goes On

As mentioned earlier, the Institute's 100th Anniversary apparently passed unnoticed. The Newcastle Players were not prepared to let a similar thing happen when the 150th Anniversary came along.

Work on cleaning up the interior was only partially complete and all that had been done about the floor was to remove a few rotten floorboards in the corner at the kitchen end. But, on Saturday, 10th January 2009 we held an Open Evening at the Workshop to celebrate its 150th Anniversary; to let Newcastle Players members see the stage the Workshop Team had reached in refurbishing the interior of the building; and to give people who grew up in Hartshill in 1930s, 1940s, 1950s and 1960s an opportunity to revive memories of the building where they attended the Brownies, Guides, Youth Club, Saturday night dances and so on, and to share their memories with us – particularly with a view to inclusion in this book.

The event was publicised in the Hartshill & Harpfields Residents Association newsletter, the Hartshill Parish Magazine, *The Sentinel* and on BBC Radio Stoke's *Breakfast* show, and there was a steady stream of visitors throughout the evening.

The first persons through the doors – even before the official starting time of 7.30 – were brothers Brian and Graham Yelland. Brian spent his working life as an international cabaret artist and he came to see again the building where he had given his first public performance as a teenager (see page 33).

The Yellands were closely followed by Mike Allen, the grandson of the Rev. Reginald Wyatt.

John Pedrazzini brought along the register of members of the youth club from 1961 and some Newcastle Players members were amused to see me scampering around after him as he dashed around the building explaining where youth club members paid their weekly subs through a hatch just inside the front door, where the amplifier, speakers and record deck where set up, and where they had staged the Hartshill version of the popular BBC Television programme of that time *Juke Box Jury* with the Vicar's wife on the panel.

My neighbour Barbara Goodwin also came along to revive memories of the building. Her father Leonard Tulley was one of the Churchwardens who signed the conveyance transferring ownership of the building from the Church to the Newcastle Players and, for many years before that, as Church Treasurer,

The Lord Mayor and Lady Mayoress of Stoke-on-Trent, Councillor Derek Capey and Mrs Joyce Capey, with our President Elizabeth Rowley, Chairman Rob Vaughan and Life Member Jim Ward at the Open Evening to celebrate the 150th Anniversary of the Workshop on Saturday, 10th January 2009.

Photograph by Richard Slater

he had been heavily involved in overseeing the Institute's finances.

The most distinguished visitors were the Lord Mayor and Lady Mayoress of Stoke-on-Trent, Councillor Derek Capey and Mrs Joyce Capey, who had earlier been to the Britannia Stadium to see Stoke hold Liverpool to a 0-0 draw but came along to spend the rest of the evening with the Newcastle Players. Councillor Capey has been a member of the Mitchell Memorial Youth Centre Committee for some years, but during his year of office as Lord Mayor he has to stand down. However, he is still a staunch supporter of the theatre and, through that, the Newcastle Players. In fact, before he left, thanking us for inviting himself and Mrs Capey to our Open Evening he said that he would like to repay the compliment and invited a party of Newcastle Players to visit him in the Lord Mayor's Parlour.

More visitors might have attended the Open Evening but for two competing events: the Stoke match and the pantomime *Cinderella* being staged in Penkhull Village Hall by the Hartshill, Penkhull and Trent Vale

Some of the visitors and Newcastle Players members chatting and enjoying a glass of wine during the Open Evening. There was also Coca-Cola and other soft drinks available.

Photograph by Richard Slater

Players. That is certainly where the Vicar of Hartshill was performing, as evidenced by a photograph in *The Sentinel* of the previous evening.

The visitors were able not only to refresh their memories of what the building was like when it was the Hartshill Church Institute but also to see how the small team led by John Hough and Rob Vaughan has been refurbishing the Workshop's interior. They also heard how we propose to replace the rotten timber in the floor at the kitchen end and then to cover the whole floor with hardwearing plywood to recreate a flat surface. After that painting of the walls will be completed.

Back to its main purpose

That done the building will revert to what has always been its main purpose: building the sets for our productions at the Mitchell Memorial Theatre in Hanley. However, it should be said that the Mitch – as we commonly refer to the theatre – is itself about to undergo a major refurbishment – its first in fifty

It's said that a ghostly figure appears on the balcony at the top of the spiral staircase (see next page). But has anybody actually seen it?

years – and it will not be available to us to use until possibly the end of 2010 or even early 2011. In the meantime we will be performing at The Rep in Leek Road, Stoke thanks to the cooperation of our friends at the Stoke-on-Trent Repertory Theatre.

12. The Institute Ghost

As mentioned on page 60, when the Newcastle Players bought the Institute from the Church in 1969, our then President, John Barstow, regaled us with a tales of a ghostly figure which was reputed to pass through the wall from the adjoining cottage and stand on the gallery looking down on what was going on down below.

Nobody who has used the building since then has actually seen this ghost – maybe because, until Newcastle Players member Pat Mason recalled the story recently, nobody else was aware of it. Obviously a case of 'What you've never known, you never miss'. Or does that mean that people will now start seeing the ghost?

Similarly nobody who contacted me with memories of the Church Institute volunteered information about the ghost. On the other hand, when asked if they knew anything about it, several recalled having heard stories about the ghost when they were younger.

The question remains: Who is the ghostly figure? I can think of two possibilities:

1. It is the ghost of the original occupier of the house next door, now known as Campbell Cottage, 289 Hartshill Road. He was Thomas Hill, described in the 1861 census as a china figuremaker, then 55 years old and born in Derbyshire.

   or

2. Colin Minton Campbell himself, keeping an eye on what the building he financed 150 years ago is being used for today.

I repeat: Will people start seeing the ghost again, now that they know about it?

13. The Sting in the Tail

The sting in the tail or perhaps it should be "sting in the tale" was the question of funding for the publication of this book. As I said earlier, in 2006 we met representatives of the Heritage Lottery Fund who, while not being able to help with the renovation of the building, suggested that a book about its use over the years would be of value and that the fund might assist with financing its publication.

Having spent some time on research and having written enough of the book to be certain of the viability of the project, I contacted the Heritage Lottery Fund again. The person I spoke to was most enthusiastic about the progress I had made but said that it was not the sort of thing the fund financed directly. For that I would have to contact Awards for All, a joint Lottery grants scheme aimed at local communities, supported by – amongst others – the Heritage Lottery Fund.

From the Awards for All website I downloaded *Awards for All Guidance Notes*, a 21-page document telling me what Awards for All would do and what it would not do. I was encouraged to read that "the application form is short and simple". In fact it ran ran to twenty-one questions and – with further guidance notes, a page of tick boxes and details of the supporting documentation required – it was only two pages shorter than the guidance notes.

Another drawback was the statement: "We will not fund . . . projects that take place or start before you receive our award letter". In other words, having embarked on the research and written part of the book – at the suggestion of Heritage Lottery Fund officials – we had disqualified ourselves from an award.

Maybe there is some way round that but, in view of our experience of devoting a lot of hard work and incurring considerable expense on our unsuccessful Lottery bid, we felt that there was no point spending any more time or effort on pursuing the Awards for All route.

So, we have published this book using our own resources. We hope that it has interested you or, better still, brought back some happy memories of the building – whether you know it as the Hartshill Church Institute or the Newcastle Players Theatre Workshop – and we hope that sufficient people will buy the book to enable us to recover our outlay and make some money which will go towards our fund for the refurbishment of this Grade II Listed Building.

Appendix A
The Workshop Workers

Over the past four decades the workshop has been kept going by a small and dedicated team of workers. Never more than a handful, some stay for just a play or two, others give years and years of service. Every so often there is a plea for more helpers. There have been times when this was because the older ones wanted to retire. At other times it was because the new, young helpers had now moved on to university or left the district for some other reason.

Nevertheless, the team has somehow kept going.

On the next few pages I have included photographs of some – but by no means all – of the people who have worked at the workshop since 1969. To those I have missed out I apologise. It is just a case that I do not have photographs of everybody involved.

I also apologise to anybody caught at a less than flattering angle. The fact is that nearly all the photographs were taken as people worked to avoid interrupting what they were doing. None of them are studio portraits.

We are, however, very grateful to everybody who has lent a hand at the workshop over the years. Without them we could not have produced all those shows at the Mitchell Memorial Theatre.

Arthur Gennery, Pat Mason, Bill Stevens and Peter Tunstill. The three in white coats are workers. Peter is just a visitor.

Photograph by courtesy of Staffordshire Sentinel News & Media

Alan Keeling and Bill Stevens working on the set of "Outside Edge", our Golden Jubilee production in 1984.

![John Whittaker and Simon Thompson photograph]

John Whittaker and Simon Thompson.

Alan Davies.

Ben Devall.

Tom Farrington.

Brett Edwards.

Pat Mason adjusting a door.

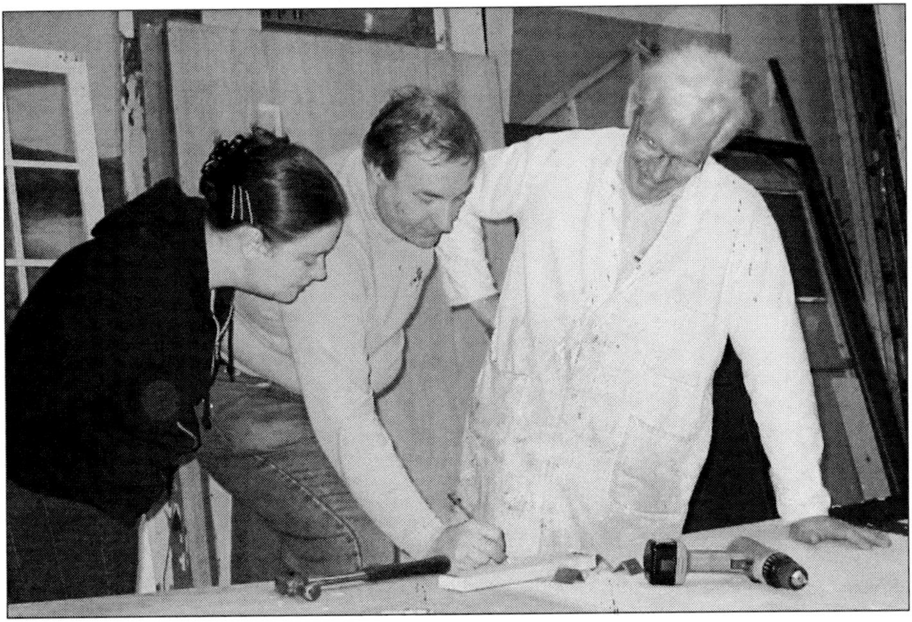

Vicky Broad, John Hough and Charles Miller.

Chris Hammond and paint pot.
Photograph by Rob Vaughan

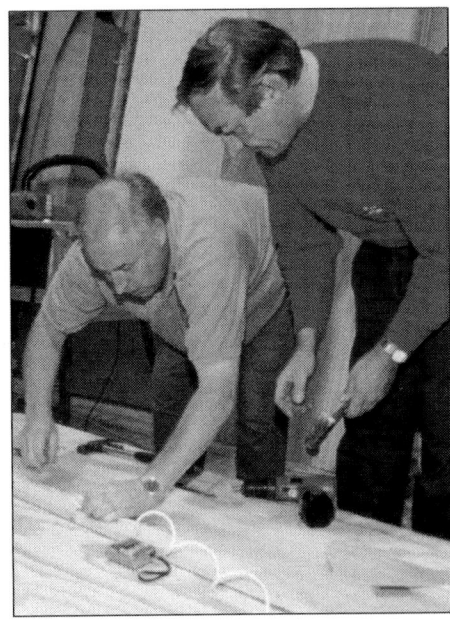

Vic Grieve and John Hough.

Mick Gould and Louise Shore with another paint pot.

Photograph by Chris Hammond.

Sylvia and Mike Fisher painting a backcloth.

Some of the team who worked on the latest refurbishment of the workshop: Rob Vaughan, Helen Farrington, John Hough, Pat Austin and Mick Gould.

Photograph by Rob Vaughan

Appendix B
The Sets

Since 1969 – or 1970 to be more accurate – we have presented 78 full-length plays at the Mitchell Memorial Theatre. And the set for every one of these plays was assembled and erected first at the workshop. Sets come in a variety of shapes and sizes. The simplest takes the form of a room with one wall missing so that the audience can see what is going on inside it; i.e. just three walls – with or without doors and windows. Other sets are more complicated with a wealth of doors and/or windows. They may require stairs and sometimes even an upper floor. Then there are plays which call for a split set showing two or more locations. The ultimate example of this as far as the Newcastle Players are concerned was *'Allo 'Allo* (2003) which, quite apart from having twenty characters, takes place in nearly as many different locations. This really tested the set designer's ingenuity and required the creation of a whole range of mini-sets within the main basic set.

Some examples of these various sets – but by no means all 78 – are shown on the following pages.

By the way, it should be borne in mind that, although the sets take several weeks to create in the Hartshill workshop, they have to be transported to the Mitchell Memorial Theatre and rebuilt on the stage there in a matter of hours. Again this is a tribute to the dedication and skill of our workshop team.

Although the first set to be built at the workshop was for *Midsummer Mink* which staged at The Mitch in April 1970, we unfortunately don't have a photograph of it in our archives. In fact the earliest for which we have a photograph is our 1980 production of *Wait Until Dark* which opens our selection of set photographs.

"Wait Until Dark" (1980). The actors in the foreground are Ian Batt, Ann McArdle and Bob Freeman. Angela Booth is the character seen in silhouette at the top of the stairs.

"Who Killed Santa Claus" (1988): a set with an upper floor containing a landing and bedroom doors.

"Beyond Reasonable Doubt" (1994). The First Act was set in the Central Criminal Court (The Old Bailey). The actors are Bob West, Richard Stevens, Aline Lewis and Elizabeth Rowley.

The Second Act of "Beyond Reasonable Doubt" called for a totally different set: the living room of Sir David and Lady Metcalf's house in Wimbledon, complete with staircase and landing.

"Double Cut" (2001) was set in s Spanish villa. Note the 'marble' floor and grand piano, the latter kindly loaned by J. Tostevin & Son of Hartshill.

The cast of "Party Piece" (2002) pose for the Sentinel photographer. This play was set in the back gardens of a pair of semi-detached houses, the garden on the left of the picture paved with concrete slabs, the other a lawn with flower beds.

One of the several mini-sets required for "'Allo 'Allo" (2003). This one is Café René. Two British airmen hid from the Germans in the space behind the clock over the door.
Photograph by Rob Vaughan

The action of "Out Of Focus" (2003) took place in the less than glamorous setting of a village hall. The actresses are Jill Bowdery and Vicky Broad.
Photograph by Rob Vaughan

Founded 1934 – The Story of the Newcastle Players

Founded 1934 – The Story of the Newcastle Players, also by Geoff Price, traces the history of the society from its beginnings seventy-five years ago, performing first in church halls and later in the Municipal Hall in Newcastle-under-Lyme before moving to the Mitchell Memorial Theatre, Hanley in 1958.

The 180-page book contains a wealth of illustrations and information about productions, people and places that have played an important part in the story of the Newcastle Players through eight decades.

Proceeds to workshop refurbishment fund

The proceeds from the sale of the book are going to the fund which the Newcastle Players have set up to pay for the ongoing refurbishment of the society's Theatre Workshop in Hartshill, Stoke-on-Trent.

The book is available direct from Geoff Price, at 103 Paris Avenue, Newcastle, Staffs. ST5 2QP at £9.95 (plus £1.50 to cover second class postage and packing). Cheques should be made payable to G. H. Price.